YOUR RETIREMENT
MONEY

HOW TO MAKE IT LAST

To Russell Coffee

Phil McCracken

PHILIP G. McCRACKEN, Ph. D.

B & G PUBLISHING COMPANY
GREENSBORO, NORTH CAROLINA

YOUR RETIREMENT MONEY

HOW TO MAKE IT LAST

Published by:
B & G Publishing Company
P.O. Box 4046
Greensboro, N.C. 27404

Printed and bound in the United States of
America

First Edition

        YOUR RETIREMENT MONEY
        How to make it last

        Bibliography
        Index

ISBN 0-9633349-0-5

DISCLAIMER

B & G Publishing Company and the author shall be neither responsible nor liable for any damage or loss caused or alleged to be caused, to any person or entity, directly or indirectly by the information contained in this book.

It should be understood the publisher and author are not engaged in rendering legal, accounting, tax, or other professional services. If these services are needed, the advice of professionals should be obtained.

Every effort has been made to make the book as accurate as possible. However, errors in type and content may still exist. The text is intended as a general reference and to complement other retirement planning information. Some of the information is up-to-date only to the time of publication.

ACKNOWLEDGMENTS

Many individuals, knowingly and unknowingly, contributed to this book. I would like thank Mr. Bill Cleveland, Mr. Chet Milligan, and Mr. Steve Holbrook of Holbrook Keeton Capital Management, who read early versions of this book and made many useful suggestions. I would also like to thank Dr. Paula Kaiser for editing the manuscript and for suggestions on arrangement to a final form.

YOUR RETIREMENT MONEY

TABLE OF CONTENTS

CHAPTER			PAGE NUMBER
	INTRODUCTION		1
1	MONEY AND RETIREMENT		5
2	YOUR ASSETS		11
3	YOUR INCOME		25
4	YOUR EXPENSES		45
5	BALANCING INCOME AND EXPENSES		59
6	REDUCING EXPENSES		69
7	SOCIAL SECURITY		81
	A	RETIREMENT BENEFITS	82
	B	DISABILITY BENEFITS	94
	C	SURVIVOR BENEFITS	97

8   MEDICAL INSURANCE/MEDICAL COSTS   101

    A   PRIVATELY INSURED   102
          MEDICAL PLANS

    B   MEDICARE   108

    C   NATIONAL MEDICAL CARE COSTS   114

    D   SUMMARY OF MEDICAL COSTS   116

9   INSURANCE   119

10   TAXES   131

11   OTHER FINANCIAL TOPICS

    A   EARLY RETIREMENT INCENTIVE   155
          OFFER
    B   SHOULD YOU DRAW SOCIAL   163
          SECURITY AT AGE 62?
    C   INCOME FROM INVESTMENTS   166
    D   SPENDING PATTERNS OF THE   168
          ABOVE AGE 65 POPULATION
    E   POPULATION TRENDS IN   174
          THE UNITED STATES
    F   COMPARISON OF TAXED AND   177
          TAX DEFERRED SAVINGS
    G   ADVANTAGE OF TIME IN   179
          SAVINGS
    H   FIRST WITHDRAWALS FROM   181
          ALREADY TAXED SAVINGS
    I   REVERSE MORTGAGES   185
    J   COST OF OWNERSHIP OF   187
          NON-PRODUCTIVE ASSETS

    CONCLUSION   193

    REFERENCES   195

APPENDIX A   GENERAL FINANCIAL TABLES   199

    A-1   DESCRIPTION OF FINANCIAL   200
           TABLES
    A-2   COMPOUND VALUE OF $1.00   203
    A-3   SUM OF AN ANNUITY   204
           $1.00 FOR N PERIODS
    A-4   PRESENT VALUE OF $1.00   205
    A-5   PRESENT VALUE OF AN ANNUITY 206

APPENDIX B   HISTORICAL FINANCIAL DATA 211

    B-1   HISTORIC INFLATION RATES   212
    B-2   HISTORIC INTEREST RATES   213
    B-3   HISTORIC RETURN ON STOCKS   214

APPENDIX C   MISCELLANEOUS ATTACHMENTS 215

    C-1   LIFE EXPECTANCY IN THE   216
           UNITED STATES
    C-2   JOINT AND LAST SURVIVOR   217
           LIFE EXPECTANCY
    C-3   LIFE EXPECTANCY FOR   218
           ANNUITIES
    C-4   1986 TAX SCHEDULE   219
           (10 YEAR AVERAGING)
    C-5   10 YEAR AVERAGING TAX   220
           TABLE
    C-6   VALUE OF WAITING TO   221
           DRAW SOCIAL SECURITY

APPENDIX D   FINANCIAL EXAMPLES   223

    D-1   BALANCING INCOME AND   224
           EXPENSES
    D-2   ESTIMATING SOCIAL   239
           SECURITY BENEFITS
    D-3   INSURANCE CALCULATIONS   248

INDEX   257

YOUR RETIREMENT MONEY

INTRODUCTION

If you are ready to retire or have already retired, but feel you have been negligent in saving enough, this book is for you. This book will show you what to do to make your money last the rest of your life.

Retirement is great. Sleep late. No Bosses. Do what you want to do, whenever you like. This sounds great but there may be just one little problem, money.

I retired several years ago. I thought I understood the economics of retirement. I had problems in matching income with expenses. To help solve my own problems, I took on a study of the financial side of retirement. I found there was a shortage of information taking into account inflation and life expectancy. I developed methods for analyzing real life situations to arrive

at ways to balance income and expenses
over a projected lifetime. I'm hoping
the results of my study and experience
will help others to live satisfactorily
on the assets they now have.

This book will show you how to use
your total nest egg to get an income that
accounts for inflation and life
expectancy and that will last the rest of
your life. This income becomes the upper
limit for your expenses. If expenses are
higher than income, you must make
reductions in spending. This book shows
you how to assign savings to expense
reductions so you meet your financial
goals.

The specific steps are:

1.   Develop your list of assets
2.   Calculate the income over your
     lifetime from these assets.
3.   Estimate your annual retirement
     expenditures.
4.   Find the gap between your income and
     expenditures.
5.   If this gap is negative, find
     reductions in living costs that will
     bring your expenditures in balance
     with your income.

The methods of calculation should be
useful to those with a high degree of
financial sophistication as well as those
who have trouble balancing their
checkbooks. Many examples are included
to serve as patterns for different
situations.

This is not a book about the
psychological and philosophical aspects
of retirement. Many such are available.

This is not a book on how to invest your money. Everyone in the world claims to be an expert at this and wants to relieve you of some of it. This is not a book to tell you how to save for retirement. There are many of these. This is a "how to" book about the financial aspects of retirement at the time of and after retirement.

Only a few people have enough money to live in retirement with the same standard of living they had while working. We never seem to save enough. There are hundreds of books on pre-retirement planning. We heard throughout our lifetime the words "Save for retirement." In spite of this barrage of information we most likely saved some, but not as much as we had hoped.

Most people retire with the feeling they must reduce their spending to handle the lower income of retirement. They probably don't know how much they must reduce their spending. They probably have heard they can live on 60 to 80% of their current spending. They haven't given much thought to inflation or medical insurance costs. Today they know interest rates can drop to levels that haven't existed for many years.

In spite of the barriers to retirement 1,500,000 people will retire in the United States this year. There are over 30 million people in the United States over 65 years of age, most of whom are retired. These new retirees and the old hands are getting by on what they have. You can too. But, it might be less stressful if you know what you are facing and how to handle it.

CHAPTER 1

MONEY AND RETIREMENT

Money is essential for retirement.
At the point of retirement our income
producing days are over and we must live
on what we have. Not only that, we must
live the rest of our lives on what we
have. This book shows you how to do
this.

I retired several years ago from a
large corporation with a moderate
retirement incentive package. This
incentive package, when combined with
other normal retirement benefits, seemed
like plenty of money. Interest rates
were high, so when I balanced my needs
against my calculated income, as I
perceived them at the time, it appeared I
could live the way I had been living. I
looked around for some data on things
like interest rates, inflation rates, and
cost of living. The data located on
these cursory searches was not what I
needed. Since I wasn't totally happy
with my job, and since I thought I could
live the way I had been living, I took

the plunge. Then reality set in. The stock market quit going up and even plunged precipitously. Interest rates dropped and inflation kept rising. I could not reduce my spending the way I thought I could. The nest egg that was to last 20 to 30 years was disappearing at a rate such that it would be gone within a few years. At this point I decided that I should reevaluate my position. I took on a major study of the economics of retirement.

This book presents my financial findings, experience, and information so that others considering retirement or in retirement can evaluate their financial positions. Many examples are included to serve as patterns for different situations.

THIS IS A FINANCIAL BOOK

This is a "how to" book about the financial aspects of retirement at the time of and after retirement. This book shows you how to find out how long the savings will last, and what you should do to make them last the rest of your life.

How long your money will last depends upon how much you have and how fast you spend it. This statement is simple but is the key to evaluating your financial position. Some people may not have choices on income. It may be fixed in the form of pensions and Social Security. Other people may have mainly cash equivalent assets that can be converted to income at times they choose.

Whatever your situation, you probably
wish you had more.

"HOW TO" STEPS OF THIS BOOK

These steps were listed in the
introduction but are repeated here for
emphasis.

1.   Develop a list of your assets
2.   From these assets calculate your
      income. This income must account
      for inflation, interest rates, and
      your life expectancy.
3.   Estimate your annual expenses.
4.   Find the gap between your income and
      expenses.
5.   If this gap is negative, find
      reductions in living costs that will
      bring your expenses in balance with
      your income.

Essential to your evaluations are
estimates of inflation, interest rates,
and your life expectancy. Later chapters
will show you exactly how to incorporate
these items into your information. Your
opinions on interest and inflation rates
may be as good as those of anyone else.

The following examples give the
reasons you must account for inflation
and interest.

INFLATION

A relatively low inflation rate
of 4% per year lowers the purchasing
power of $1.00 by 50% in 18 years. An

inflation rate of 10% lowers the purchasing power of the same $1.00 by 50% in just 7 years. Since 1970 we have had five years where the inflation rate was above 9% and 6 years under 4%. Only two years were at or under 3%. The average over the 21 years (1970 through 1990) was 6.2%. Thus, $1.00 of purchasing power in 1970 would buy only 28 cents worth of goods by 1991. Most people near retirement age are expected to live 20 or more years, so that inflation must be a serious concern to you and considered in your evaluations.

MEDICAL COSTS

Medical costs in the United States are out of control. In the 10 years 1981 to 1990, they almost doubled (94%). The rate of increase averaged 8.1% per year. General inflation over this same time averaged 4.6% per year. Your financial plan must give careful attention to this increasing cost of medical care.

INTEREST

An interest rate of 7% will double the value of an asset in 10 years and quadruple it in 20 years. An interest rate of 12% will more than triple the value in the same 10 years and bring it to 9.6 times the value in 20 years. These points may influence how you invest your money.

BACKGROUND INFORMATION

One of the purposes of this book is to provide historical information that can help you look into the future. Several key items of information are:

1. Historical inflation rates.
2. Historical interest rates and rates of return on various types of investments.
3. Cost of living increases for Social Security benefits.
4. Life expectancy.

Chapters are also devoted to Medical Costs, Social Security benefits, Insurance, Taxes, and a series of miscellaneous topics. Many of these items are essential to your decisions and will be useful in developing strategies for financial survival after retirement.

SUMMARY

The methods of calculation are very general. You balance your assets and income against the expenditures you expect. This sounds very simple but can take a large effort just to collect the data you will need. You may have to spend hours, days, or even weeks collecting the information.

Since the view of the future is not clear, you must make decisions on approximate information. This can be done provided you have considered all major factors. The main point is: get

clear on your earning assets and on the
income that you expect from these assets.

The hardest part of the entire
exercise is to balance your projected
income and expenses. You may be forced
to make very difficult decisions on your
projected life style. The cuts are
usually in the luxury area on items such
as second automobiles, vacation homes, or
frequency of dining in your favorite but
expensive restaurant. This will force
you to set priorities on spending that
may not have been necessary before.

Most people think about retirement.
Some people want to retire as young as
possible. Others may intend to work
their entire lifetime. Most of us are
somewhere between. We don't mind working
but have other things we would like to
do. Some people simply take a different
job, often for less income, but with much
greater satisfaction. Frequently, if you
have the option of leaving a job it is
easier to stay with it. Financial
independence relieves many worries and
takes away a huge burden. Most people
would just like the financial
independence to be able to say "TAKE THIS
JOB AND SHOVE IT" even if they stay where
they are.

CHAPTER 2

YOUR ASSETS

Corporations and businesses develop two types of financial statements. One is the profit and loss statement covering a period of time. The second is the financial position of the company on a certain date. This is often called the Balance Sheet and shows both assets and liabilities.

This chapter is devoted to showing you how to get a list of your assets. The next two chapters are devoted to calculating your income and your expenses. All will be similar to that of a corporation.

YOUR ASSETS DETERMINE YOUR INCOME

Your "Net Assets" may be called your "Net Worth." Your net worth is your total assets less your total liabilities. In this chapter we will address the net worth you have now, or will have after your retirement. We will use the words "Net Worth" and "Net Assets" to mean the same thing. An "Asset" is an item in

your list of assets. The main purpose
for developing your net worth is to use
it to project your income after
retirement. Not only do assets produce
income but they also can be consumed as
living expenses during retirement. Some
types of assets even can consume income.

"Assets" as used here are those
items you own that are worth money.
Assets include the usual cash items such
as checking and savings accounts, IRA's,
and insurance. They also include items
in which you have a right to benefits.
Examples are: the union or company
pension, life insurance benefits
guaranteed by companies, and medical
benefits from medicare or your company.

When you retire, there may be a loss
of benefits. Examples of these are total
or partial loss of medical care benefits
from your company, loss of life
insurance, and loss of the use of a
company car. These losses must be noted
so that you can make the decisions
whether to replace at your expense.
These will add to your financial need.

Some assets that you have may be
worth money, but there may be no reason
to convert them to cash. Furniture in
your house has a value, but since you
probably will need it most of your life,
it is not an income generating asset. If
you stop housekeeping, and sell
everything for cash, the furniture then
would be an asset.

Your Net Worth list must include all
income generating assets and all assets
that could be converted to income. Since
this list is to be used to calculate your

income over your lifetime, it must be complete.

ORGANIZATION OF YOUR ASSET LIST

There are many ways of organizing this information. I have found it convenient to separate the information into two types of categories, money assets and other assets.

Money assets are those assets readily converted to cash or those which can earn income or both. These include checking and savings accounts, CD and money market funds, IRA's, stocks, bonds, and notes held. Also in this category are items such as rental property, real estate, or other items that generate income or convert to cash.

The rights that accrue to you on retirement or on reaching a certain age are a major asset for most people. These are items such as pensions, Social Security, Medicare, or company medical plans.

Some items may be in one or the other category depending on your point of view. For example, a coin or stamp collection may have significant value, but your intention of selling it signifies what type of asset it is.

Some minor benefits come by virtue of age or retirement. For example, some businesses give reductions to AARP members or to those over 65. Some country clubs reduce dues for members after long years of membership and at a

given age. Breaks for being retired are
often given on automobile and home
insurance. These will not show up on your
asset list but show as a reduction in
your living expenses.

        A sub-section of the money assets
must include a list of debts that you
have. This includes items such as home
and automobile mortgages, credit card
debts, home equity loans, and other
financial commitments. You must have a
complete understanding of your debts,
since most debts must be repaid. Debt
repayment will increase the income you
will need.

CHECK LIST OF YOUR ASSETS

INCOME GENERATING ASSETS

a.   Checking accounts
            Yours
            Your spouse's
b.   Savings Accounts
            Yours
            Your spouse's
c.   Other Cash Items
            Certificates of Deposit
            Money Market Funds
            Money due from others
            Insurance policies (Cash values)
d.   Securities
            Stocks
            Bonds
            Trusts
            Limited Partnerships
            Mortgages held
            IRAs

e.   Entitlements (Income Rights)
         Pensions from work place
         Military Pension
         Social Security
         Annuities
f.   Income Property
         Rental Housing
         Rental Equipment

OTHER ASSETS

a.   Housing
         Primary home
         Second Home
         Time Share rights
b.   Household Goods
         Furniture (Primary Home)
         Furniture (Secondary Home)
         Other Furniture
c.   Automobiles
         Primary
         Secondary
         Other Vehicles
d.   Collectibles
         Stamp collections
         Coin Collections
         Paintings
         Art Objects
         Antique Furniture

DEBT AND OTHER LIABILITIES

a.   Mortgages and long term debt
         Primary Home
         Second Home
         Other Real Estate Mortgages
         Second mortgages
b.   Short Term Debt
         Automobile Notes
         Credit Card Debt
         Home Equity Loans
         Personal notes owed

c.   Other Financial Commitments
      Promises To Pay
      Personal Commitments to children.

VALUE OF YOUR PENSION

In this chapter it is not necessary for you to know the value of the entitlements you have, if you know the income they will generate. However, you may want to estimate the value of these items to put them in perspective with the other assets you have. In addition, the value of these entitlements will be necessary in the calculation of the size of your total retirement kitty. Chapter 5 describes this in more detail.

We now come to the first financial calculation. Since this is typical of many to follow you should take the time to understand it. It will be used in much of this book. Two terms must become clear to you. These are "Annuity" and "Present Value of an Annuity." This understanding is necessary since the calculations require that you know the "Present Value" of your pension or Social Security benefits. The definitions are:

An Annuity is a plan where a sum of money is set aside and invested so periodic payments can be made in the future. Payments may begin immediately or deferred to the future.

The Present Value of an Annuity is the amount of money set aside today, drawing interest at a specific rate,

to pay out periodic payments for a
specified number of years.

Appendix A-5, Table 1 is an annuity
table that shows the amount of money
needed today --Present Value-- to provide
fixed future payments of $1,000 per year.
The interest rate and the number of years
the payments are to be made must be
specified.

Another concept you must understand
is that of payment escalation. If you
wish to maintain a standard of living you
must increase the amount you receive each
year to allow for inflation. For
example, Social Security payments have
increased by an average of 4% per year.

The tables of Appendix A-5 differ.
Table 1 gives a fixed payment over the
years. The others (Tables 2 to 8)
escalate the payments by 4, 5, 6, 7, 8,
9, and 10% per year, which covers the
range of expected inflation. In all
cases, the payment is at the end of the
year.

The following example illustrates
the use of these tables. If you have a
pension paying you $1,000 per year for 20
years, the Present Value of an annuity
will be the value of this entitlement.
You will find a value of $9,818 from
Table 1 of Appendix A-5 (8% interest, 20
years). If the pension payments amount
to $10,000 per year, the present value
will be 10 x $9,818 or $98,180.

COMPOUNDING OF INTEREST

The time value of money is another thing you must consider. Money, when invested, earns interest. Most investments earn compounded interest. That is, the interest is added to the principal after each period of time. Throughout this book we have used one year as the compounding period. (Savings accounts often use a quarter of a year as the compounding period). For example, $1,000 invested at 8% becomes $1,000 x 1.08 or $1,080 one year later. If this money is kept in this investment for another year, it becomes $1,080 x 1.08 or $1,166.40. After three years the amount is $1,166.40 x 1.08 or $1,259.71.

It is easy to get the result from Appendix A-2. This table, called the "Compound Value of $1.00," gives the figures for compounded interest. Look down the 8 percent interest column at 3 years and find the value of 1.2597. Multiplying by $1,000 gives the value of $1,259.70. This same figure is (1.08) x (1.08) x (1.08) x $1,000.

The calculation is handled another way with the use of Appendix A-4. This table gives "Present Value of $1.00." This is the amount of money, invested at a given interest rate and for a given time, that will result in $1.00. From the table, 8% interest and 3 years, we find a value of 0.7938. Using the situation above, $1,259.70 x 0.7938 gives $999.95 (more decimal points would give $1,000). These calculations are illustrated by examples.

UNDERSTAND YOUR PENSION OR ANNUITY

EXAMPLE 1

You have an annuity purchased some years ago that will pay fixed payments of $2,500 per year. Say that it begins to pay you at age 65 (your current age) and will pay for the rest of your life. Assume that you will live for 20 years. Since insurance companies are conservative, use 6% interest. From Table 1, Appendix A-5, find the value $11,470 (6% interest, 20 years of annual payments). This is the sum needed today for each $1,000 of annual payments for the next 20 years. Taking 2.5 times this number gives a value of $28,675 that is necessary to provide $2,500 per year.

If you are not yet 65, the cash value will be less by the amount of interest the principal will earn between now and the date you will start drawing payments. Assume that it will be 3 years before you begin to draw on this annuity.

The present value will be:

$28,675 / {(1.06)x(1.06)x(1.06)}
= $24,076.

The value of (1.06) x (1.06) x (1.06) is the compounded sum of $1.00 given in Appendix A-2. Under the 6% column and for three years, we get a figure of 1.1910. Dividing $28,675 by 1.1910 gives the same $24,076.

Another way to calculate this is to get a multiplying factor from table A-4 in the appendix "Present Value of $1.00" (0.8396 for 3 years at 6%). This figure, multiplied by $28,675, again gives $24,076.

EXAMPLE 2

Assume you have calculated your Social Security benefit at $8,000 per year. Social Security payments escalate at near the inflation rate. Assume an average inflation rate of 4% per year, an interest rate of 8% per year, and a life expectancy of 20 years. Table 2 of Appendix A-5 gives a value of $13,247 per $1,000 of annual initial benefit. Multiplying this figure by $8,000/1000 or 8 gives $105,974. This is the amount of money that must be invested and earn 8% interest to pay $8,000 per year (inflated by 4% per year) for 20 years.

Most company pensions and other privately paid pensions do not escalate for inflation, or escalate at a rate much lower than the inflation rate. Some of my friends have pensions that escalate at the inflation rate while pensions of others do not.

DOES YOUR PENSION

ESCALATE WITH INFLATION?

Besides illustrating how to make the calculation on the value of an entitlement, this exercise shows you have a net worth higher than you think. More importantly it forces you to find out

more about your pensions. Do they
escalate or are they fixed? If they
escalate, what are the formulas used to
set the escalation rate? Chapter 11,
Section A discusses the evaluation of
your pension as part of an early
retirement offer. AARP, Reference 1, has
a useful free book available called "A
GUIDE TO UNDERSTANDING YOUR PENSION."

Since we are on the subject of
annuities, the tables of Appendix A-5 can
be used to calculate a figure for the
value of earning assets you must have to
get a given annual income. Since,
inflation of at least 4%, and interest
rates of about 8% are prevalent, an
income of $30,000 per year in 1992
dollars will require a total nest egg of
about $400,000. This will be discussed
in more detail in later chapters.

YOUR FINAL ASSET LIST

The asset check list previously
given, and the form (Table 2-1) at the
end of this chapter can be used to get a
list of assets with total values for the
various categories. Also at the end of
this chapter is an example (Table 2-2) of
a completed asset list. Yours may be
simpler or more complex and you may have
more or fewer assets. The essential goal
is to get your assets listed in a form
you understand and **you** can manipulate as
you see fit. (Computer spread sheet
programs make it very convenient). If you
are like many of us, it may be necessary
to move assets from the "Other category"
to the "Earning asset" category. In other
words you don't want to be "land poor."

That is, own assets worth money but have little money for your daily needs.

Referring to Table 2-1, I have included three sub-categories under "CASH EQUIVALENTS". These are called: 1. LIQUID ASSETS, 2. NON-LIQUID ASSETS, and 3. ENTITLEMENT ASSETS.

Liquid assets are those you could convert to cash within a few weeks. Non-liquid assets are those that may require years to convert to cash. Entitlements are those that generate a periodic income but cannot be converted to cash. Money, invested in IRA's, Keogh's, 401K's, is normally your money, but a 10% tax penalty is assessed if withdrawn before you are 59.5 years old. Thus, if you are under 59.5 years of age, some of your assets may be in the non-liquid category.

TABLE 2-1

SAMPLE WORK SHEET

CALCULATION OF ASSETS

DATE —/—/—

```
CASH EQUIVALENTS
LIQUID ASSETS
   Checking Accounts .......$ _____
   Savings  Accounts .......  _____
   Money Market  .........:.. _____
   Certificates of Deposit .  _____
   IRA .....................  _____
   401k ....................  _____
   Keogh/SEP ...............  _____
   Saving Bonds ............  _____
   Stocks/bonds w/ Broker ..  _____
   Insurance cash value ....  _____
   Due from XXX ............  _____
   Other cash assets........  _____
            TOTAL         $  _____
NON-LIQUID ASSETS
   Sale of business ........$ _____
   Limited partnerships.....  _____
   Rental property .........  _____
   Note due from xxx .......  _____
            TOTAL         $  _____
ENTITLEMENTS
   Company pension .........$ _____
   Social security .........  _____
   Health Insurance.........  _____
            TOTAL         $  _____
TOTAL CASH EQUIVALENT     $ _____

OTHER ASSETS (NOT CONVERTED TO CASH)
   Primary home ............$ _____
   Second home .............  _____
   Automobiles .............  _____
   Collectibles.............  _____
            TOTAL         $  _____

     TOTAL CASH + OTHER    $ _____

DEBT
   Business debt............$ _____
   Home mortgage............  _____
   Automobile mortgage......  _____
   Rental prop. mort........  _____
   Credit card debt.........  _____
            TOTAL DEBT    $  _____

TOTAL   (CASH+OTHER)-DEBT  $ _____
```

TABLE 2-2
SAMPLE ASSET LIST

TOTAL ASSETS JANUARY 1, 1992

```
CASH EQUIVALENTS LIQUID ASSETS
    Checking Accounts          $ 3,000
    Savings  Accounts            5,000
    Money Market                20,000
    Certificates of Deposit     35,000
    IRA                         32,000
    401k                        59,000
    Keogh/SEP                   48,000
    Savings Bonds                3,000
    Stocks/bonds w/ Broker      78,000
    Insurance cash value         2,500
    Due from company             1,800
               TOTAL          $287,300

NON-LIQUID ASSETS
    Sale of business           $50,000
    Limited partnerships         4,000
    Rental property             48,000
    Note due from xxx            2,500
               TOTAL          $104,500

ENTITLEMENTS
    Company pension            $125,000
    Social security             105,000
    Health Insurance             20,000
               TOTAL          $250,000
    TOTAL CASH EQUIVALENT      $641,800

OTHER ASSETS
    Primary home               $125,000
    Second home                  39,000
    Automobiles                  18,000
    Collectibles                 37,000
               TOTAL          $219,000
        TOTAL CASH + OTHER    $860,800

DEBT
    Business debt              $ 50,000
    Home mortgage                62,000
    Automobile mortgage           9,000
    Rental prop. mortgage        39,000
    Credit card debt              3,500
               TOTAL DEBT     $163,500

TOTAL {(CASH+OTHER)-DEBT}     $696,500
```

CHAPTER 3

YOUR INCOME

Your income after retirement is the
key to your future. At the time of
retirement your income becomes less
flexible. The savings have been saved.
Your pensions and Social Security are
there. You either know or will soon know
what they will be. You may have some
loose ends to fix up such as sale of a
business or property, but in essence your
financal future is fixed.

This chapter will show you how to
estimate what you can expect as income
after you retire. You have listed and
classified your assets in the previous
chapter. These assets form the basis for
your income. The next chapter will show
you how to develop ideas about your
estimated needs.

For the fortunate few there will be
no problem. Your income will exceed your
needs and you can still leave some for
your children to spend wisely, save, or
squander as they see fit. This brings up
an important decision you must make. Do
you really want to leave a significant
part of you assets to your children? The

decision is easy if your income from your assets supports your life style without depleting assets. If you are like many of us you may have to spend some of your assets to live in your latter years. You may have seen the bumper sticker "WE'RE SPENDING OUR CHILDREN'S INHERITANCE." This is a fact for most of us.

To calculate your income, you have to make some estimate of when you will retire and some guess of how long you will live. When to retire is easy. Some people will retire as early as possible, others will work as long as they are able. The range of years you intend to continue to work is small. It generally won't vary by more than 5 years. However, the years you will live is not up to you and may be much longer than you think.

WHEN WILL YOUR RETIRE?

The term "Retirement" is relative. It is generally taken to mean you have left the job or work that was your main source of income, and that you do not intend to work full-time in the future. You may still wish to do some part-time work for money. Many retirees do some part-time work for money for at least a few years after retirement.

If you are working for a corporation you probably will retire between the ages of 55 and 65. The laws state you may work as long as you wish, but only few people continue to work for the other person past age 65. If you are self-employed you may work significantly longer.

The facts are, the laws, rules, regulations, and customs are geared to people retiring between 59.5 and about 65 years of age. You cannot draw money out of qualified plans such as IRA's, 401K's and SEP or Keogh funds without penalty before 59.5 years of age. Social Security retirement benefits do not start before age 62 and Medicare does not begin until age 65. Countering this are the actions of many large corporations who go through the exercise of offering retirement incentive packages. These are to entice people to leave their employment before normal retirement age, simply to reduce the number of employees. These retirement incentive packages are normally designed to help cover the financial gap until the standard retirement benefits begin.

There are two general types of retirement plans. These are: Defined Benefit and Defined Contribution. You must know what yours is and its details. In the past, most were benefit defined in which you would know exactly what the benefits would be. Contribution defined plan benefits depend on how well the investments of the program did over the years. Many companies are now using benefit defined plans.

RETIREMENT AGE AFFECTS
YOUR PENSION BENEFITS

Most defined benefit pension plans lead to a retirement income at age 65 of about 50% of your last year's income or average of last 5 years or so of income. If retirement occurs earlier than age 65, there is normally a reduction in pension benefits. This figure is generally around 3% to 5% for each year under age 65. (For Social Security, the reduction is 6 1/3% for each year under 65.) Thus, retirement at 55 would mean a reduction in benefits of at least 30% from a level that is generally about 50% of the last year's salary. In this case you would draw only 35% of your last year's salary. Therefore, there must be significant "other income" to maintain a viable standard of living.

Another option that may be available with your pension is the assignment of benefits to your spouse for his/her lifetime as well as yours. A typical reduction is 20% in benefits, in return for the pension lasting through both lifetimes.

If your rich uncle died and left you a large inheritance, you may be in great financial shape. If you have been very successful in business or in the stock market, you may be financially secure. If you had a very effective savings program, you may have adequate assets to meet long term needs. However, if you are like many of us where spending rises to meet our income (C. Northcutt

Parkinson passed a law on this), early
retirement may be only a dream.

Many people use the accrued
benefits from a company plan to allow
them to take another job which may pay
less money but give greater job
satisfaction. If this is your goal, it
will be very useful to you to go through
the same studies as if you were retiring.

As you go through the actions to
estimate your income for a given year's
retirement and find it inadequate, you
might plan for a later year and develop a
saving plan aimed at that year. This
would have the fallout effect of lowering
your spending habits which tend to carry
into retirement. Lowering your spending
is the same as increasing your income or
assets. The annuity tables in Appendix
A-5 show that a lowering of spending by
$1,000 per year reduces the saving
required for retirement by $15,000 to
$18,000.

HOW LONG WILL YOU LIVE?

No one on this earth can tell you
how long you will live or how long your
spouse will live. What we can say is how
long the average person of your age is
expected to live. Even this is not very
satisfactory because an average means
that you have a 50% chance of living
either longer or dying earlier. This is
a gruesome subject for many people, but
it is necessary to pick a number for the
number of years you and your spouse
expect to need an income.

Statistics on life expectancy as
given by the Bureau of Labor Statistics
are in Appendix C-1. This table shows
the expected years a person will live
from the current age. The data were
developed in 1986. A few years are
summarized below:

LIFE EXPECTATION, YEARS

AGE IN		WHITE		BLACK	
1986	TOTAL	MALE	FEMALE	MALE	FEMALE
45	32.9	30.4	35.8	26.4	32.2
50	28.5	26.1	31.2	22.7	28.0
55	24.3	21.9	26.8	19.3	24.0
60	20.4	18.2	22.6	16.1	20.3
65	16.8	14.8	18.7	13.4	17.0
70	13.6	11.7	15.1	10.8	13.9
75	10.7	9.1	11.8	8.7	11.1

These data do not reflect several
factors that can increase or lower the
life expectancy of an individual. Major
factors are: if you smoke, are married,
the longevity of your parents, and your
general health and frame of mind. People
who do not smoke live, on the average 6
years longer than those who do. If you
are married you will live 3 years longer,
on the average, than those who are not.
If you have a positive outlook on life,
you may extend your life by 5 years. If
your parents had a very long life, you
can expect to live 2 to 4 years longer
than the average. With all the positive
things in your favor you can easily
expect to live to a ripe old age and beat
the averages by many years.

PEOPLE LIVE LONGER TODAY

In the last 20 years the population in the United States increased by 23%. The population of people over 65 years of age increased by 36%. The number of people over 85 years of age increased by 89% and the number of people of 100 years of age increased by 100%. We're living longer! A very significant portion of the people now in the 55 to 65 year-old range will live to the ages of 85 or older.

The percentage of total population in the above age 65 category, who are 85 years old or older has increased from 5.6% in 1960 to 9.7% in 1988. This proportion is expected to increase to 13.3% by the year 2000. Today, medicine is just entering the "Biological Age" of gene modification with the promise of cures for many major diseases and prolonged life. Many of these will come to fruition in the next ten to twenty years or within your projected life time.

The gist of this is that you probably will live longer than you think. You make your decision on the years to put into your calculations, but if you are now 55 to 65 years of age, it seems prudent to assume you will live to be 85 or 90 years old. I know several people who are retired (age 60 to 70) who have at least one parent still alive (85 to 100 years old). The children of these old timers probably will live longer than their parents since this has been the case for many years now. Chapter 11,

Section F shows population trends in the United States.

HOW LONG WILL A NEST EGG LAST

To illustrate the need for spreading your income from assets over your life time, consider the following tables. These tables show the time in years that a sum of $10,000 will last. For example, an annual withdrawal of $1000 escalated at 5% per year will deplete a principal of $10,000, drawing interest at 8 %, in 12.7 years. Withdrawals are escalated according to inflation after the first year.

8% INTEREST ON PRINCIPAL

INITIAL	INFLATION, %				
WITHDRAWAL	0	4	5	6	7
$ 500	INFINITE	40+	32.5	27.3	23.1
$ 750	INFINITE	20.2	18.2	16.3	15.3
$1,000	20.9	13.5	12.7	11.9	11.3
$2,000	6.6	5.9	5.8	5.7	5.5
$3,000	3.8	3.7	3.7	3.7	3.7

10% INTEREST ON PRINCIPAL

INITIAL	INFLATION, %				
WITHDRAWAL	0	4	5	6	7
$ 500	INFINITE	40+	40+	40.+	33.1
$ 750	INFINITE	28.7	23.6	20.6	18.5
$1,000	INFINITE	16.7	14.8	13.8	12.9
$2,000	7.3	6.4	6.2	6.0	5.8
$3,000	4.2	4.0	3.9	3.9	3.8

YOUR ESTIMATED INCOME

There are many ways to develop your estimated income but there are several

points to consider in your income list.
Some are:

1. Will the income last through your
   lifetime?
2. Will the income last through your
   spouse's lifetime?
3. Are incomes escalated for inflation?
4. Are assets being depleted,
   maintained or increased?
5. Are the incomes taxed, tax free or
   partially taxed and have the proper
   tax rates been assumed?
6. If you are under 59.5 years of age
   are surtax penalties in effect on your
   income?
7. Are the interest rates you assumed
   reasonable?
8. Are the inflation rates you assumed
   reasonable?

   In Chapter 2 you saw how to get a
list of your assets. This list of assets
has items from which you can expect
income. One item not shown on this asset
list is your ability to supplement your
income by part time-work.

HOW TO ORGANIZE

YOUR INCOME INFORMATION

   The ideal type of retirement
financial plan would be to list for every
year of your and your spouse's futures,
your income, your expenses, and remaining
assets. This could be done, but since
your crystal ball is probably like mine,
cloudy and murky, and worn down to the
size of a marble, it is probably not

worthwhile to go through the exercise in that extreme.

Most people will find it necessary to list only the first two or three years of retirement. Your income list will be different from anyone else's. Below are three tables to give you an idea of possible variations. You can easily have your own variation or you may use more than one for different puposes. Table 3-1 is the most flexible with income shown from different sources. The next table (3-2) may be important to you if you have a split between fixed income and discretionary incomes.

Another way of organizing your income information is by the degree the income is taxed. (Table 3-3) You may have some income that is fully taxed, some partially taxed, and some not taxed at all. Since it is to your benefit to withdraw already taxed funds first, this may be a better way for you to see what happens over several years. See Chapter 11, Section I.

TABLE 3-1

ITEM	1992	1993	1997	NOTES
FIXED INCOME				
Company Pension				
Other Pensions				
Social Security				
Annuities				
INCOME FROM SAVINGS				
Tax Deferred plans				
Taxed Savings				
Life insurance				
Other				
INCOME FROM BUSINESS				
Rental Income				
Sale of Business				
Deferred Profits				
OTHER INCOME				
Earned income				
Earnings from mortgages				

TABLE 3-2

ITEM	1993	1994	1998	NOTES
FIXED INCOME				
Social Security				
Company pension				
Employee Annuity				
Rental Income				
Earnings from Mortgages				
DISCRETIONARY INCOME				
Tax deferred savings				
Taxed Savings				
Sale of Business				
Deferred Profit Sharing				
Earned Income				

TABLE 3-3

NOT TAXED OR SLIGHTLY TAXED
  Stocks/bonds
  Insurance withdrawals
  Sale of business
  Savings
  Annuities
  Mortgage repayments

TAXED OR MOSTLY TAXED
  Social Security
  Company pension
  IRA withdrawals
  Tax deferred withdrawals
  Earned Income

DATA COLLECTION IS IMPORTANT

A reliable estimate of your income will require a serious effort on your part. Some parts of your income will require information from other organizations.

You may not know the amount you can expect from Social Security, from your company pension, or from other type annuities you may have. A separate chapter is provided on Social Security benefits. You may use this intimidating chapter to calculate the exact benefit or you can go straight to the Social Security office. Allow several weeks to hear from them.

You may be familiar with your company's pension plan. If not, contact the Employee Benefits group of your company. They don't have to know you are thinking of leaving. Just tell them you

are interested in knowing your vested
position. I can assure you they often
get these requests. Again, depending on
the type of plan, this may take some
time.

Company provided annuities are like
the above. You may have to go directly
to the company or the insurer, which
again will take time.

If you have any special sources or
potential sources of income such as
trusts, they should be identified and the
tax situation determined.

Collecting the data can take many
weeks and much hard work on your part. I
suggest you get familiar with the topics
of Social Security, Medical costs,
Insurance, Taxes and the Financial topics
described in Chapters 7 through 11.
These should help you do a better job of
estimating your income.

If you are like many others, you
have the ability to shift income between
years, to delay taking some benefits, and
to some extent to decide between taxed
and untaxed incomes. The notes on the
assumptions you used will be necessary
when you try to resolve the conflict
between income and expense. You must
expect to revisit your table of income
many times as you balance your income and
needs.

TAXES ARE AN IMPORTANT FACTOR

Taxes play a major role here.
Almost everything will swing on the tax

situation.   Chapter 10 is devoted to
taxes that are important in reaching a
retirement decision.   It does not attempt
to cover the entire tax law.   A few key
points are repeated here.

1.   Money drawn from tax exempt or
tax deferred plans cannot be
withdrawn before age 59.5 with
out paying a 10% tax penalty.

2.   Withdrawals must begin from tax
deferred accounts by age 70
1/2.

3.   Money can be taken from
accounts that have already been
taxed without paying tax.   Only
the income from these accounts
is taxed.

4.   Annuities are often purchased
with money that has already
been taxed.   Thus, the income
from annuities may be only
partially taxed.

5.   There are various situations
where lump sum distributions
are made.   When these are
taken, you are faced with a
decision on whether to pay
taxes on the lump sum under
special rules, or to draw out
as needed and only pay taxes on
the amount withdrawn.

USE ALREADY TAXED MONEY FIRST

Illustration of a hypothetical case
for the effect of drawing money from

already taxed accounts first, instead of tax deferred accounts, is shown with calculations in Chapter 11, Section I.

Start with $100,000 in a tax deferred account and $100,000 in a taxed account. Assume both earn interest at 8% a year. From the total of $200,000 draw out enough to have $15,000 per year after paying taxes. Assume a marginal tax rate of 15% and an interest rate of 8%. Assume funds are withdrawn at end of year to make the calculations easier. All relevant taxes are paid at the end of the year.

CASE 1. Withdraw funds from tax deferred account first and then transfer to the already taxed account when funds from the tax deferred account are depleted.

CASE 2. Withdraw funds from the taxed account first, letting the tax deferred account grow until the taxed fund is exhausted.

Table 3-4 given below summarizes the results from Chapter 11, Section I. The amounts shown for the various years is the amount of money remaining after withdrawing $15,000 plus taxes each year.

TABLE 3-4

TOTAL VALUE OF ACCOUNTS

	CASE 1	CASE 2
INITIAL	$200,000	$200,000
AFTER 5 YEARS	186,631	199.749
AFTER 10 YEARS	163,405	202,493
AFTER 15 YEARS	141,133	194,623
AFTER 20 YEARS	110,186	182,438
AFTER 25 YEARS	67,186	164,534
AFTER TAX (25 YRS)	67,186	128,336
TOTAL TAX (25 YRS)	58,544	84,726

In the particular situation illustrated here, there is an after-tax gain to you of $61,150 over the 25-year period, by drawing taxed funds first. You should make every effort to exercise this principle in practice.

DO NOT SPEND ALL OF YOUR

DISCRETIONARY MONEY IN

YOUR EARLY RETIREMENT YEARS

A very important point to consider here is if you have significant assets other than pensions and Social Security. Income can easily be shifted from one year to another. This is a double edged sword, since you may deplete these savings in your early years and leave nothing for later years.

For a preliminary estimate of income from savings, go to Appendix A-5, Table 2 and get the value of $16,942/$1,000 of current withdrawal (4% inflation, 8% interest, 30 years). Divide this figure into your current savings to get the income you can expect in the first year. This income will increase each year by 4%.

SAMPLE INCOME STATEMENT

Table 3-5 is an example of a simple income statement. This table has an assumed need. The income from various categories are lumped together to make the table short. You should be able to do about the same thing. An interest rate of 8% was used.

A table such as this can show: your income needs, your sources of income, your total assets or at least key assets, and key information to calculate taxes for the given period. More detailed analysis on this type of income and spending plan will be covered in Chapter 6, which is concerned with balancing income and spending.

TABLE 3-5

NEED	1992	1997	NOTES
Estimated need	$50,000	$60,800	1
INCOME			
Social Security	$8,400	$10,200	1
Company Pension	24,000	25,000	2
Stocks, Bonds, Savings, Initial amount $150,000	17,600	25,600	3
From tax Deferred plans. Initial value $200,000	0	0	4
Total income	$50,000	$60,800	5
Estimated Taxes	4,466	3,974	
ASSETS			
Savings.	$150,000	$ 99,815	
Tax deferred plans	200,000	293,865	
Total assets	$350,000	$393,680	

NOTES:
1. Inflate 4% per year.
2. Totally taxed.
3. Tax on interest paid each year.
4. Tax paid on amount withdrawn each year.
5. Includes taxes

The ideal situation is to have one table showing your needs without taxes, your income from fixed sources, the taxable part of these fixed income sources, the assets, the interest on the assets, withdrawals from assets, adjustments to income, deductions from income, and taxes due. This can be done

if the lists of assets are not too
extensive or if they are lumped into
categories as above.

Doing this for many years is not
precise because so many things change.
The tax structure changes almost every
year, inflation rates and interest rates
can change frequently, so that at best
you have only an estimate for the future
years. And without a computer it is
almost too much work. However, it is
necessary to consider the future even if
we must assume many things will stay the
same. We must assume we will have needs
in the future that are similar to what
they are now.

Chapter 5 will show how to look at
your income for future years. You will
be able to develop incomes based on
different interest and inflation rates.

CHAPTER 4

YOUR EXPENSES

This section is to help you estimate
how much money you will need to live on
in the future. Since we are talking
about the future, it will be only an
estimate, but it is a necessary element
to aid you in deciding if you can afford
to retire on your expected income.

The most straight forward way of
doing this is to start with your current
year's expenditures, which will be
adjusted to predict your future financial
requirements. The adjustments will
eliminate savings, reduce taxes, and
reduce any other expenditures that seem
possible. There may be increases in such
things as travel and hobbies. For most
couples, the predicted future expenses
will be 60 to 80% of the last working
year's expenses.

You may be the type of person who
has a well defined budget with all
expenses itemized and good records. Or,
you may not know what you spent last
year, let alone know what you spent on
the various items. Most of us are
somewhere between the two extremes.

EXPENSE CHECK LIST

Table 4-1 is a detailed check list that will satisfy most people. There will normally be something unusual that will require modification. Most expenses can be put into major need categories as follows:

Housing	Insurance
Food	Club dues
Clothing	Savings
Medical and Dental	Mortgage Payments
Transportation	Business expenses
Entertainment	Gifts
Vacations/travel	Alimony
Taxes	Child care
Charity	Other major items

A common situation is where two members of the family have incomes with different types of expenses. In addition, one member may continue working after the other retires. Major need categories may be different from these given above.

Table 4-1 on the next page gives a more detailed check list.

ORGANIZATION OF DATA

As with your assets and income, there are many ways to organize your data. The main point is to get it into a form that you understand and you can easily manipulate. In my case I tried several layouts on different sizes of tables. I finally found it was more convenient to develop several tables which had the same list of expenditure items and the last full year's expenditures on these items.

If you wish to follow this plan, each table will contain columns with your expenditures by item (first two columns from your left). For one table, a third column will contain tax deductions for these expenditures. Other columns might list areas where reductions or increases in cost of living are likely to occur. You may be contributing to saving accounts, Keogh funds, or employee savings plans, which might be in a column called "To equity." Other columns may be for groups such as Business expenses, Second home, and Automobiles. These tables, when properly developed, can be very useful when you are trying to estimate your future expenses. It will be used to identify areas where cutting expenses may be possible. Table 4-2 and 4-3, are examples of two expense tables.

IT MAY TAKE SEVERAL YEARS TO

LOWER YOUR INCOME TO YOUR

FINAL RETIREMENT EXPENSES

The second table (Table 4-3) should include the same expense items and the same expenses as the first table but with other columns reserved for future year's expenditures. Surprisingly, it may take several years to reduce some of your expenses. First, not everything happens on January 1 or the day after you retire. Second, you may have commitments that go

for several years. For example, there
may be commitments to the son or daughter
still going to college, but will be
leaving after graduation or the
commitment to your church for the next
three years. If you are in business for
yourself, it may take several years to
clear it up to the point that your income
tax liabilities no longer exist. A
particularly long-range estimate of
expenses will be necessary if one or the
other of a married couple plans to
continue working for several years.

     To analyze further your current and
future needs, you may break down the
major categories into sub-categories
similar to table 4-1.   The main thrust
here is to get all expense items listed.
A special category called "Miscellaneous"
may be included to cover unknowns and the
difference between what you spent and
itemized expenses. This figure should be
as small as possible without making your
lists unduly long. This figure seldom
will be zero and must not be negative.
For accurate projections it would be
desirable to have this figure less than
10% of the total.

USE MAJOR CATEGORIES:

DO NOT HAVE TOO MUCH DETAIL

     Don't forget that the purpose of
this exercise is to estimate your future
needs. It is not necessary to have
expenses itemized to the nearest penny.
Looking into the future is hazy, so your
goal here should be to get the data in a
form that you understand and can make

judgments of your future needs on a particular item.

"WHAT IF?" QUESTIONS

If you have several "What If?" questions, you may want a third table similar to table 4-3 but with columns for the different "What If?" situations. Some potential questions that families might ask, are:

1. What if we moved to a rental apartment from our current home?
2. What if we moved to a cheaper, smaller home?
3. What if we had fewer automobiles?
4. What if we sold the vacation home?
5. What if we paid off our debt?

Tables can be developed to show the impact of this type of item on the current year's and future year's expenses. Your family expense patterns, the complexity of your spending, and the number and type of possible changes will dictate how you should set up your expense tables. The idea is to make them fit your situations.

PLAN FOR UNEXPECTED OR

MAJOR OCCASIONAL EXPENSES

Every household has non-routine expenses. Some may be planned, such as a new car. Others may be unexpected, such

as the need for a new water heater in
your home.

This type of expenditure must be
included in your financial plan. You
probably have some idea of your past
experience. For example, how often do
you get a new car? Do you keep your
automobiles longer, but with occasional
unexpected maintenance costs? What about
the major appliances? If your children
are setting up housekeeping, they may
prevail on you if they over extend their
finances.

At the end of this chapter are
sample tables giving an itemized list of
expenditures. A "miscellaneous" item is
included which can include this type of
expenditure.

In my case I include some under
automobile maintenance, some under
houshold maintenance, and some under the
miscellaneous category. I just know that
the unexpected always happens.

TAXES PLAY A MAJOR ROLE

If you review the example tables at
the end of the chapter in some detail,
some items may confuse you. The tables
were set up to capture all income and to
make it easier to calculate the estimated
income tax. Note that the federal income
tax was the biggest item on the list and
that total tax amounted to about 29% of
the total income in the first year but
only 21% in the second year. In the
cases presented here, it was assumed that
the total income was taxed with some

normal types of deductions. Your
situation may be different. For example,
one half the Social Security benefit is
taxed unless your total income is below
certain levels. Also taxes may not have
to be paid on money withdrawn from
accounts containing money that has
already been taxed. When considering
your future financial requirements you
cannot neglect the impact of taxes.
Chapter 10 covers taxes that are
important at retirement, but does not
attempt to cover the normal on-going tax
laws.

UNDERSTAND YOUR EXPENSE TABLES

On Table 4-2 you see a listing for
depreciation and capital loss. These show
no impact on income but do affect the tax
deduction column. Thus, it is reasonable
to include items on your list that have
an impact on tax. This will be
particularly important if you or your
spouse is self employed, if you have a
business on the side, or if you have
significant trades in the stock markets.

A column was included on the cost of
your primary home. It was assumed there
is still an outstanding mortgage on the
home. This is common since many people
move later in life and since mortgages of
25 to 30 years are standard. Chapter 11
has information on the true cost of this
home. Interest on the mortgage and
property tax is deductible, but you must
pay tax on the other home expenses and
there may be little financial return on
your investment.

Table 4-2 has a column showing the amount of your income that goes toward increasing your total net worth. As you retire, you probably will stop most of your savings. In this table there were contributions to a company 401K plan and stock purchases from earnings.

Again, as discussed above, you should develop the table for your needs. Columns showing the amount spent on categories such as entertainment, business expenses, insurance may be important in your case. These columns should only be for major categories, particularly if they may be candidates for reducing expenses.

No prorating of income taxes to the categories was done here. If this were done, you would get a better picture of the true cost of some of your categories that may be candidates for reduction.

FUTURE SPENDING

In the tables shown here, most items were escalated 4% per year except medical and dental costs that were escalated 8% per year. Home mortgage payments and alimony are normally fixed payments. Some of your spending patterns will change. For example, you will have more time for hobbies and travel. You may do more repair work around home. You may decide to do your income tax filing. In projecting expenses to the future, you may decide to cash in your life insurance policy. You may decide to move some dividend-paying stock to a tax exempt situation or live your early years of retirement on money that has already been taxed.

In the next chapter we use projected future living expenses as a basis for balancing your income and expenses.

TABLE 4-1

CHECK LIST OF EXPENSE ITEMS

Housing
  Mortgage
  Utilities
  Maintenance
  Major additions
  Insurance
Transportation
  Payments
  Operating cost
  Major maintenance
Food
  Meals at home
  Meals eaten out
Entertainment/related
  Travel
  Movies, etc.
  Dues
  Gifts
Medical/dental
  Insurance
  Drugs/prescriptions
  Dental
Contributions
  Church
  Gifts
Business expenses
  Personal business
  Income business
Taxes
  Federal income
  State income
  Intangible
  City taxes
Other Expenses
  Clothing
  Child Support
Savings
  Stock Purchases
  Saving accounts

Second home
Time share condo
Special maintenance
  or remodeling
Property taxes

Bus fare
Insurance
Taxes

Business meals

Hobbies
Alcoholic beverages
Tobacco
Magazines, books

Special items
Medical deductible

Political

Property
FICA
User fees

Life Insurance
Alimony

Retirement plans
IRA contributions

Your situation may have many others.

TABLE 4-2
EXPENDITURES

ITEM	1992 EXP.	TAX DED.	HOME COST	TO EQUITY
HOUSING				
MAIN HOME	5964	3707	5964	2257
TIME SHARE	475	0	0	0
UTILITIES	2500	0	2500	0
INSURANCE	400	0	400	0
MAINTENANCE	500	0	500	0
AUTOMOBILE				
PAYMENT	2707	0	0	2196
OPERATIONS	1300	0	0	0
INSURANCE	600	0	0	0
MAINTENANCE	500	0	0	0
FOOD				
DINE OUT	1000	0	0	0
DINE IN	3000	0	0	0
CLOTHING	1500	0	0	0
MEDICAL	600	0	0	0
DENTAL	200	0	0	0
LIFE INSURANCE	1250	0	0	0
CHARITY	1000	1000	0	0
HOBBIES	500	0	0	0
ALIMONY	3600	3600	0	0
ENTERTAINMENT	700	0	0	0
TRAVEL	1000	0	0	0
GIFTS	1000	0	0	0
KEOGH/401K	4500	4500	0	4500
STOCK PURCHASE	5000	0	0	5000
MARGIN INTEREST	800	800	0	0
REINVESTED DIV's.	1000	0	0	1000
BUSINESS EXPENSE				
OUT OF POCKET	1000	1000	0	0
DEPRECIATION	0	700	0	0
CAPITAL LOSS	0	1000	0	-1000
FINANCIAL EXPENSE	400	0	0	0
MISCELLANEOUS	4000	0	0	0
TAXES				
FED. INCOME	8358	0	0	0
STATE INCOME	4202	4202	0	0
FICA	4398	0	0	0
PROPERTY	2100	2100	0	0
INTANGIBLE	75	75	0	0
TOTAL	66129	16307	9364	13953

TABLE 4-3
EXPENDITURES

LAST WORK YEAR AND YEARS FOLLOWING

EXPENDITURES	1993	1994	1995	1995
HOUSING				
MAIN HOME	5964	5964	5964	5964
TIME SHARE	475	494	514	534
UTILITIES	2500	2600	2704	2812
INSURANCE	400	416	433	450
MAINTENANCE	500	520	541	562
AUTOMOBILE				
PAYMENT	2707	2707	0	0
OPERATIONS	1300	1352	1406	1462
INSURANCE	600	600	624	649
MAINTENANCE	500	520	541	562
FOOD				
DINE OUT	1000	1500	1560	1622
DINE IN	3000	3400	3536	3677
CLOTHING	1500	1000	1040	1082
MEDICAL	600	648	700	756
DENTAL	200	216	233	252
LIFE INSURANCE	1250	0	0	0
CHARITY	1000	1000	1000	1000
HOBBIES	500	700	728	757
ALIMONY	3600	3600	3600	3600
ENTERTAINMENT	700	728	757	787
TRAVEL	1000	1040	1082	1125
GIFTS	1000	1000	1000	1000
KEOGH/401K	4500	0	0	0
STOCK PURCHASE	8000	0	0	0
MARGIN INTEREST	800	0	0	0
REINVESTED DIV's	1000	0	0	0
BUSINESS EXPENSE				
OUT OF POCKET	1000	0	0	0
DEPRECIATION	0	0	0	0
CAPITAL LOSS	0	0	0	0
FINANCIAL EXPENSE	400	0	0	0
MISCELLANEOUS	4000	4000	4000	4000
TAXES				
FED. INCOME	8358	4192	3834	3973
STATE INCOME	4202	2670	2775	2845
FICA	4398	0	0	0
PROPERTY	2100	2184	2271	2362
INTANGIBLE	75	75	0	0
TOTAL	66129	43126	40842	41835

TABLE 4-4

WORK SHEET

CALCULATION OF EXPENSES

ITEM	199X EXPENSE	TAX DEDUCT	HOME COST	TO EQUITY
HOUSING				
MAIN HOME				
TIME SHARE				
UTILITIES				
INSURANCE				
MAINTENANCE				
AUTOMOBILE				
PAYMENT				
OPERATION				
INSURANCE				
MAINTENANCE				
FOOD				
DINE OUT				
DINE IN				
CLOTHING				
MEDICAL				
DENTAL				
LIFE INSURANCE				
CHARITY				
HOBBIES				
ALIMONY				
ENTERTAINMENT				
TRAVEL				
GIFTS				
KEOGH/401K				
STOCK PURCHASE				
MARGIN INTEREST				
REINVESTED DIVIDENDS				
BUSINESS EXPENSE				
OUT OF POCKET				
DEPRECIATION				
CAPITAL LOSS				
FINANCIAL EXPENSE				
MISCELLANEOUS TAXES				
FED. INCOME				
STATE INCOME				
FICA PROPERTY				
INTANGIBLE				
TOTAL				

CHAPTER 5

BALANCING INCOME AND EXPENSES

By this point you have developed your list of assets, projected expenses, and income for at least the first year of your future. This chapter will show you how to project your expenses and income for the rest of your life. These projected expenses will include the effects of inflation. The projected income will cover the needs of this inflation.

The main goal of this chapter is to measure the gap between expense and income over the rest of your life. You will either have an income that is adequate or you will find a negative gap between income and expense. If you have this negative gap, don't feel like the lone ranger. Most of us are in this category. Most people who have retired in the past were in this situation and survived. If the gap is negative, the figure will serve as a goal for your cost reduction efforts.

This gap will help answer two questions: "Will what we have last until we die?" and "How much do we have to cut our living expenses so the answer to the first question is YES?"

The answers to these questions require knowledge of your income, expenses, and assets. In addition, you must understand how inflation will increase your needs and how return on investment rates will influence your nest egg.

INFLATION

The following table illustrates how inflation eats away at our spending dollar. It shows how much money you will need to have $1,000 of purchasing power after the selected number of years, at the given inflation rate.

TABLE 5-1

YEARS	INFLATION RATE				
	4%	5%	6%	7%	8%
0	$1,000	$1,000	$1,000	$1,000	$1,000
5	1,217	1,276	1,338	1,403	1,469
10	1,480	1,629	1,791	1,967	2,159
15	1,801	2,079	2,397	2,759	3,172
20	2,191	2,653	3,207	3,870	4,661
25	2,666	3,386	4,292	5,427	6,848
30	3,243	4,322	5,743	7,612	10,063

This table shows that even with a modest inflation of 4% per year, after thirty years we need three times as much money as in the first year to buy the same amount of goods. The $2.00 box of

cereal today may cost $6.00 to $12.00
twenty-five to thirty years from now. I
remember as a child a hair cut was 35
cents. Today, I pay $11.00 for the hair
cut and I'm bald. APPENDIX B-1 gives the
purchasing power of the dollar (U.S.
Bureau of Labor Statistics) since 1951.
In that period of 40 years, the value of
the dollar dropped by a factor of 5. In
other words, a 1951 dollar is now worth
only $0.20. The average inflation rate
over this long period was 4.1% per year.

COMPOUNDED INFLATION

The data as given in APPENDIX A-2
were used to construct TABLE 5-1. If you
take the case of 6% compounded for ten
years, APPENDIX A-2 gives a figure of
1.7908. Multiplying this by $1,000 gives
$1790.80. From TABLE 5-1 we see a figure
of $1,790.85 for $1,000, inflated for 10
years at 6% inflation.

Your total living costs must be
escalated by some inflation factor.
Throughout this book I have used 4% per
year, which has been a past average
number. For most people, not all costs
will escalate with inflation. For
example, a mortgage payment is generally
fixed. Therefore, the average inflation
for total living expenses is less than
the average inflation. Countering this,
you may have expenses in categories with
higher than average inflation rates. The
cost of medical care is the most
significant. I suggest you use at least
4% for inflation unless you have a firm
basis for using a lower number. You may
feel better using a higher number.

Because of this persistent inflation
and the general feeling of people in the
United States that some inflation is
good, we cannot expect a letup. Our
government policies of not balancing the
budget guarantee that we will have
inflation. The only question is: how
much? Our retirement plans must account
for inflation. This has the net effect
of requiring more initial money in our
retirement kitty.

ANNUITY TABLES

An annuity table gives the initial
sum of money needed to allow a periodic
payment for a certain length of time.
The tables in this book are for the
withdrawal of $1,000 per year. If the
$1,000 is the same over the years its
escalation rate is 0%. Since inflation
must be considered, other annuity tables
are given for different rates of
escalation. The tables of APPENDIX A-5
are for 0, 4, 5, 6, 7, 8, 9, and 10%
escalations of $1,000. These tables show
the amount of money that must be
available to provide future purchasing
power of today's $1,000, but escalated by
the specific inflation rate.

The following table gives the
initial amount needed to maintain the
$1,000 purchasing power, for 30 years, at
8% interest, and for different inflation
rates.

INFLATION RATE	INITIAL NEED NO TAXES
0%	$11,258
4%	$16,942
6%	$21,461
8%	$27,778
10%	$36,704

This very dramatic increase shows why we must include inflation in our retirement plan. The low inflation rate of 4% increases our initial asset need by about 50%. A 10% inflation rate increases the initial need by 300%.

CALCULATION OF NEED

The initial amount of money necessary to meet a given spending need, inflated over a specific number of years, can be calculated from the annuity tables of APPENDIX A-5. The following examples illustrate the use of these tables. The examples start with simple situations and go to more complex cases. In these examples we give more precise figures than may be required so that you can follow the calculations. The intent of the examples is to show you how to reach your conclusions using your information. It must be mentioned again, key words are: estimation, approximation, and judgment.

THE EXAMPLES ARE TO SHOW YOU HOW TO REACH YOUR CONCLUSIONS WITH YOUR INFORMATION

This example is the simplest of all. The couple would like to know the total assets they will need to live with a given initial income.

EXAMPLE 1

Mr. and Mrs. Doe need $30,000 to live on in 1992. They assume their joint life expectancy is 25 years. They decided to use an inflation rate of 5% per year. Their experiences on return on money has been 10% per year. They want to know what they would need if their interest rates averaged 6 and 8% instead of the 10% they have recently experienced. They expect the tax rate to remain about the same.

To maintain their standard of living, with 5% inflation a year, they will need income as listed in the following table. These figures are from TABLE 5-1 multiplied by 30 ($30,000/$1,000).

YEAR	AMOUNT PER YEAR
1992	$30,000
1997	38,288
2002	48,866
2007	62,368
2012	79,599
2017	101,590

The total nest egg they will need in 1992 is from TABLE 3 of APPENDIX A-5 (5% inflation at 6, 8 and 10% interest rates at the 25-year level). Again the figures must be multiplied by 30 for the $30,000 a year initial need.

INTEREST RATE	FACTOR 5%, 25 YEARS	TOTAL ASSETS NEEDED
6%	21,098	$632,940
8%	16,851	505,530
10%	13,749	412,470

In the following example, the retirement nest egg is composed of three parts: Social Security benefits, pension benefits, and other savings. "Other savings" includes all earning assets. For now, no attempt is made to distinguish between taxed and untaxed savings. It is assumed the "need" includes money for taxes, and the taxes increase at the inflation rate. A later example will give more details on taxes.

EXAMPLE 2

Mr. and Mrs. Smith have a need in 1992 for $40,000 a year living expenses. They have a life expectancy of 30 years. They will receive Social Security of $15,000 per year, which is expected to escalate at the inflation rate. They believe inflation will be 4% per year. They have a company pension of $10,000 per year, which is fixed and will not escalate with inflation. They would like to know how much money should be available for them to live with their current standard of living, assuming 6, 8, and 10% returns on their savings.

They set up a table showing their needs today and 30 years later.

	1992	2022
NEED	$40,000	$129,736
SOURCE OF MONEY		
SOCIAL SECURITY	15,000	48,651
PENSION	10,000	10,000
FROM SAVINGS	15,000	71,085
(BY DIFFERENCE)		

The bottom figures represent the amount they must take out from their savings each year. The withdrawals from savings escalate at a different rate from the others because the company pension does not increase. The withdrawals from savings must make up for the difference between what the company pension pays and the loss of purchasing power of the pension.

A table is set up below where the present value of an annuity for each component is calculated for the interest rates and inflation rates shown below.

		ESCALATION RATE	INTEREST RATE 6%	8%	10%
1992 NEED	$40,000	4%	$871,000	$678,000	$543,000
SOCIAL SECURITY	15,000	4%	327,000	254,000	203,000
PENSION	10,000	0%	138,000	113,000	100,000
FROM SAVINGS (BY DIFFERENCE)	15,000	?	406,000	311,000	240,000

The last horizontal row was calculated by subtracting the Social Security and pension figures from the total need. This shows the total savings required for the various interest rates.

To illustrate the method of calculation, TABLE 2, APPENDIX A-5, gives a figure of $16,942 for 4% inflation, 8% interest and 30 years. The initial need of $40,000 a year requires 40 x $16,942 or $677,680. In the table we used $678,000.

These two examples are probably the least complicated of any situation. There are many different types of situations that can be developed. Appendix D-1 gives another five examples including one showing the effect of taxes. Some of these examples cover situations in which either income or need will have significant changes after a few years of retirement.

This chapter has shown you how to calculate your required nest egg for a given initial spending need. If your earning assets are less than this need, you have a gap. You have a choice of finding more assets or reducing your spending. Since you are no longer accumulating assets, your most likely scenario is to reduce your spending. This gap becomes your goal for reduced spending. The next chapter is devoted to reducing this gap by making spending reductions.

CHAPTER 6

REDUCING EXPENSES

The last chapter showed how to
calculate your total lifetime saving
needs. From this total we deducted the
entitlements for Social Security and
pension to get the amount you should have
in savings beyond entitlements. We then
developed methods for showing whether you
have enough savings to accommodate your
life style.

YOUR RETIREMENT GAP

I call the difference between your
income and expenses the "Retirement Gap."
If this "Gap" is positive, you do not
have many problems. Your plan may need
some fine tuning, but your life style can
be maintained.

If the "Gap" is negative and you
still want to retire, you must identify
the ways you can reduce your financial
need. To do this, you need a target of
how much you must reduce your spending.
The methods of the last chapter showed
you how to estimate the size of this gap.

The reductions in spending to lower the gap must come from your list of projected expenses. Ideally, you would have a priority hit list you and your spouse agree upon. You must also know how much savings you can expect when a cut (sacrifice) is made.

Your "Gap" is probably relative. You may overcome it in the early years of your retirement at the expense of lower income in later years. Remember, you must have income the rest of your life and your spouse's life.

STEPS TO LOWER SPENDING

1. Take the items from your asset list which can produce income or which you can convert to cash. Develop an income plan that covers your life expectancy with the income increasing with the rate of inflation.

2. Take the first or second year of the plan as the basis for comparing income and need. If your gap is positive, jump up and kick your heels. If the gap is negative, don't panic, just go to the next step.

3. Use your list of expenditure categories to identify by order of priority those that you could eliminate. Assign a cost to these so that you can tell what items you must remove from your spending. These are very hard decisions to make.

GET A SPENDING REDUCTION GOAL

The table below shows the relationship between expenses and "nest egg" needs. If you reduce living expenses over your lifetime, you need less money to begin retirement.

EXPENDITURE REDUCTION DOLLARS PER YEAR	REDUCTION IN INITIAL SAVINGS TOTAL DOLLARS
$1,000	$17,000
5,000	85,000
10,000	170,000
25,000	425,000

The reduction in required initial assets is based on 4% inflation, 8% interest, and 30 year life expectancy.

OPPORTUNITIES FOR

SPENDING REDUCTIONS

There are many places you can reduce spending. The size of the gap will tell you how much you need to cut. You may reach your goal by minor reductions or you may have to make major changes in your spending habits.

A check list of items to reduce depends on your expenditure pattern, but may include the following. Develop your own reduction list.

1. Move to a cheaper home. Expenses will be less and you can convert the

difference in price to income
producing assets.

2. Sell your vacation home.

3. Sell your boat or at least give up
the docking fee.

4. Give up the country club membership.

5. Give up the second automobile.

6. Eliminate your life insurance.

7. Work with your insurance agent to
reduce the cost of your home and
automobile insurance.

8. Quit sending money to your grown
children.

9. Reach agreement with your children,
their spouses, and your
grandchildren to draw names for
Christmas and other type of gifts.

10. Reach agreement with your spouse on
spending for food and clothing.

11. Look at hobbies for saving
possibilities.

12. Do more of your home maintenance.
You will have more time.

13. Consider quitting smoking. It's bad
for you anyway.

14. Evaluate your alcohol costs. This
could be higher than you expect.

15. Review your list for items you
     consider luxury, which could lower
     your cost of living if deleted.

Reducing living expenses takes
serious efforts. Old habits are hard to
change. You and your spouse should have
the same goals. You may be changing a
major part of your life style. You have
time to do things you could not do
before. Many of these things will
require more money than you anticipated.
As a rule of thumb, you will spend more
money than you expect.

TYPICAL SAVINGS

Some typical savings possibilities
are given below with a range of savings
you might expect:

ITEM	ANNUAL SAVING		
Reduce to one automobile	$ 2,000	to	$4,000
Eliminate cablevision	250	to	500
Eliminate life Insurance	1,000	to	5,000
Do not dine out 12 times/year	400	to	700
Buy lower priced food brands	200	to	500
Never own a new car	1,000	to	2,000
Total	$4,850	to	$12,700

With tax, these items reduce the
required assets by $100,000 to 270,000.
You probably will have a different list
of things to cut, but you surely have
some that are similar.

A major pitfall for many a budget is
a failure to do quickly what you know
must be done. If you are overspending
your budget, take action now. Time is
money. Don't wait five years to do it.

Do it now. Procrastination is your enemy.

If your gap is only a small part of your spending, you may reduce it by working on the minor items. If it is 10% or higher, you probably have to go after something major.

YOUR LARGEST SAVING

A home, particularly if it is almost paid for, is a likely source of lower spending and cash. You may consider going to a cheaper home or you may consider something like a reverse mortgage described in Chapter 11. One advantage of changing to a lower value home is that you may take the once in a lifetime $125,000 tax deduction on the price appreciation. The difference in price of the homes can add to your retirement nest egg.

Some states have lower income taxes than others. For example, today Florida does not have a state income tax. Many areas of the country have lower costs of living than other areas. Rural areas and small towns generally have lower costs of living than metropolitan areas. Thus, moving to a lower cost area may have a long term benefit to your needs. Countering this will be the costs of moving, which could exceed one to two year's savings.

There are many books published on possible cost savings opportunities. Examples are: Reference 16, *Penny Pinching,* Reference 9, *How To Lower Your*

Property Taxes and Reference 5,
Understanding Your Insurance. You can
find books on almost any type of savings.
Chapter 9 on insurance, in this book,
shows some cost saving ideas when
purchasing insurance.

SAVINGS EXAMPLE

MOVE TO A LOWER PRICED HOME

Assume you have a $200,000 home and
you feel you can go to a $100,000 home.
If your home is paid for, the financial
aspects might look like this.

	$200,000 HOME	$100,000 HOME
UTILITIES	$3,000	$2,000
TAXES	2,500	1,250
INSURANCE	800	600
TOTAL	$6,300	$3,850
TAX DEDUCTION	550	275
NET ANNUAL COST	$5,750	$3,575
DIFFERENCE	$2,175	

The difference in sales price of the
two homes is $100,000. However, you must
pay a real estate fee, estimated at 6 to
7% of the sales price, and it will cost
you to make the move from one home to
another. Assume this total is $20,000.
The amount realized will then be $80,000.
This sum, added to your retirement fund,
can produce interest of $6,400 per year
if the principal remains intact. If the
sum is depleted over 25 years at 4%
inflation and 8% interest, an initial
withdrawal of $5,240 can be made, which
increases to $13,968 by the 25th year.

The swing of $2,175 in annual expenses and a gain in income of $5,240 gives a total change in position of $7,415 a year for the first year. This can make a big change in a negative gap.

This type of analysis can be made on other items such as automobiles, second homes, etc. Chapter 11, Section J has a similar calculation on the cost of owning a non-productive asset.

EVALUATION OF ALTERNATIVES

If you are trying to decide between several potential reduction items, you may put them on one table as suggested in Chapter 4. Suppose you are considering reducing to one automobile from two, and moving to a lower priced home. The automobile can be sold for $6,000, with proceeds paying off the note on the first car. The changing of homes can net $50,000, which is used to pay off the mortgage on the first home. You would like to know the impact of either or both actions on your required initial assets.

A table is set up showing the expenses for the several cases. The debt complicates the calculations, since the notes will be paid off within a few years. In each case where there is debt, a second column is shown with the debt paid off. This no-debt column was necessary since the debt could also be paid off by using savings instead of selling the item.

	CURRENT 1992	NO DEBT	SELL CAR	NO DEBT	TRADE HOME	NO DEBT	BOTH
HOUSING							
MORTGAGE	6,000	0	6,000	0	0	0	0
UTILITIES	3,600	3,600	3,600	3,600	2,400	2,400	2,400
PROP. TAXES	3,700	3,700	3,700	3,700	2,160	2,160	2,160
INSURANCE	600	600	600	600	400	400	400
MAINTENANCE	1,000	1,000	1,000	1,000	700	700	700
AUTOMOBILE							
OPER. COST	1,500	1,500	1,200	1,200	1,500	1,500	1,200
MAINTENANCE	1,000	1,000	500	500	1,000	1,000	500
INSURANCE	1,200	1,200	700	700	1,200	1,200	700
MORTGAGE	4,000	0	0	0	4,000	0	0
OTHER EXPENSES	27,400	27,400	27,400	27,400	27,400	27,400	27,400
SUB TOTAL	50,000	40,000	44,700	38,700	40,760	36,760	35,460
STATE TAXES	2,516	1,739	1,948	1,624	1,816	1,452	1,337
FED. TAXES	6,539	4,324	4,738	4,094	4,476	3,752	3,522
TOTAL	59,055	46,063	51,386	44,418	47,052	41,964	40,319

One will notice the significant impact that taxes have on the lowering of expenditures. The tax liability difference between column 1 and column 7 is $4,196 a year.

A solution to the problem is reached by calculating the assets required to maintain spending without debt and then adding the amount required to pay off the debt. However, the amount withdrawn to pay debt must include a provision to pay taxes. For purposes here, we assumed a 15% federal tax and a 7% state tax. Thus, you must withdraw $1.282 (1/(1-0.22)) from savings to pay off one dollar of debt.

Using an inflation of 4%, an interest rate on assets of 8% and a 25 year life expectancy, TABLE 2, APPENDIX A-5 gives a factor of $15,268 per $1,000 of spending.

The total assets required for the current spending are:

$$(\$46{,}063 \times 15.268) + (\$55{,}000 \times 1.282)$$
$$= \$773{,}800$$

Similarly, for the case with no car:

$$(\$44{,}418 \times 15.268) + (\$50{,}000 \times 1.282)$$
$$= \$742{,}274$$

For the trade to a lower price home:

$$(\$41{,}319 \times 15.268) + (\$6{,}000 \times 1.282)$$
$$= \$638{,}550$$

For both car sold and home traded:

$$(\$40{,}319 \times 15.268) = \$615{,}590$$

If this family has Social Security benefits of $12,000 a year and a pension of $25,000 a year (not escalated for inflation) the entitlement assets are:

ENTITLEMENT ASSETS

SOCIAL SECURITY	$183,000
PENSION	267,000
TOTAL	$450,000

The results of the evaluation are as follows:

	CURRENT	SELL CAR	TRADE HOME	DO BOTH
ENTITLEMENT ASSETS	$450,000	$450,000	$450,000	$450,000
TOTAL NEED	773,000	742,000	639,000	625,000
OTHER ASSETS NEEDED	$323,000	$292,000	$189,000	$175,000

The other earning assets are reduced by almost 50% with these two changes.

This method of analyses can be done for almost any type of projected savings, but is most useful for major changes. You can lump together smaller changes and compared with your current situation.

CHAPTER 7

SOCIAL SECURITY

This section provides basic Social Security information and the means for estimating the payments you could receive. Estimating is the key word. If you need exact amounts or if you have special or unusual situations, you should contact your Social Security office directly.

Social Security is often thought only to provide a supplement for retirement, but there are other types of benefits that can have a financial impact on your financial needs in retirement. Social Security pays four types of benefits. These benefits are:

1. <u>RETIREMENT INSURANCE</u> This is available after age 62.

2. <u>DISABILITY INSURANCE</u> This benefit is available if you are unable to work due to illness or injury.

3. <u>SURVIVOR INSURANCE</u> At your death your spouse, children, and other dependents may be eligible for benefits.

4.   <u>MEDICARE</u>   This benefit provides
hospital and medical insurance after age
65.   MEDICARE is discussed in Chapter 8,
which covers medical costs and needs.

A. RETIREMENT BENEFITS

ELIGIBILITY FOR RETIREMENT BENEFITS

You must be at least 62 years old
and have at least the minimum quarters of
contribution to the social security
system as follows:

TABLE 7-1

YEAR OF BIRTH	QUARTERS	YEAR OF BIRTH	QUARTERS
1918	29	1924	35
1919	30	1925	36
1920	31	1926	37
1921	32	1927	38
1922	33	1928	39
1923	34	AFTER 1928	40

AMOUNT OF SOCIAL SECURITY

RETIREMENT BENEFIT

Once you have decided you are
eligible for retirement benefits, you may
now wish to estimate the amount you will
receive. You may even wish to estimate
how much you will receive for different
years of retirement.

In my case I wanted to know if I
should start drawing benefits at age 62

or wait until I was older so that I could
get higher benefits. I also wanted to
know the effect on the amount of benefit
if I did not work or contribute Social
Security taxes for one or more years.
(See part B of Chapter 11).

The size of your Social Security
retirement benefit depends on the age
when you begin to draw your benefits, the
amount of your contribution to the plan
and the cost of living increases that
have increased the basic amount. An
additional factor that may be important
to your decision is the amount your
spouse or dependents might receive.

The calculations to get accurate
estimates of benefits are tedious,
require a detailed understanding of very
complex rules and regulations, and even
with a large mathematical effort will
leave you with a feeling of uncertainty.
The laws are changed frequently and
mathematical factors are revised each
year to adjust for inflation. This
requires having up-to-date information.
It is difficult to go to a Social
Security office and get general
information. The response I got was
"It's in our computers." They, however,
will do the calculations for you and are
helpful otherwise.

My suggestion is to get your Social
Security office to do the calculations
for you. They have Toll Free numbers to
call in all phone directories. If you
wish to understand the process for making
the calculations or would like to do your
own calculations, see Appendix D-2. A
very good booklet on the subject is that
of Reference 4. This booklet is updated

in December of each year to contain the next year's figures and factors.

Two terms, AIME and PIA, are used in the discussions on the amount of benefits. AIME is Averaged Indexed Monthly Earnings. PIA is Primary Insurance Amount. The AIME is based on your annual contributions and on the number of years you have contributed. The PIA is calculated from your AIME. The PIA, Primary Insurance Amount, is adjusted by age and retirement date to give your monthly benefit. The factors to get these values are adjusted each year by the Federal Government.

SIMPLIFIED RETIREMENT
BENEFITS CALCULATION

Any simplified method of estimating your Social Security benefit requires some estimate of your AIME (Average Indexed Monthly Earnings). Factors that could influence your estimate are:

1. Have you paid social security taxes most of your working life? If you are now nearing retirement age, you will need to have paid into the system for 30 to 35 years to avoid significant reductions in benefit.

2. The other major factor is the amount of Social Security taxes you have paid in. Chapter 12, Section B gives a list of the maximum amounts on which you would pay tax. As of 1992 the maximum calculated AIME is $2985 per month assuming you reached 62

years of age in 1992 and that you
intend to retire this year. If you
intend to retire three years later,
the estimated maximum AIME is $3415.

Table 7-2 shows the maximum monthly
benefit that is in effect for 1992 for
several ages. Adjust these figures for
the age at which you will actually start
drawing benefits.

TABLE 7-2

| | | | MAXIMUM | |
AGE	BIRTH DATE	YEAR RETIRE	AIME $/MONTH	PIA $/MONTH
65	1927	1992	2716	$1,028
64	1928	1992	2744	1,032
63	1929	1992	2853	1,049
62	1930	1992	2985	1,068
62	1930	1995	3415	1,133

Most people these days have incomes
that are below the maximum amount on
which Social Security tax must be paid.
Beginning in 1992 the maximum is $55,500
a year with the medical portion at
$130,200 per year. These figures are
well above the average income in the
United States. If you feel that you have
had normal increases of income over the
years, you may take the last year's
earnings to estimate your AIME.

Table 7-3 shows calculations made
for various levels of the last working
year's income. It assumes that the ratio
of this last year's income to the maximum
taxable has been constant over many
years. Thus, you may pick an income to
arrive at a value for the AIME and,
therefore, the PIA or benefit at age 65.

TABLE 7-3

RETIREMENT BENEFIT
PERCENT OF TAXED INCOME
RETIRE AGE 65   AGE 62 IN 1991

LATEST INCOME	PERCENT MAXIMUM	AIME	PIA	PERCENT OF TAXED INCOME
55,500	100%	$2985	$1068	23.0%
53,400	96.2	2871	1051	23.6
50,000	90.1	2689	1024	24.6
45,000	81.1	2420	984	26.2
40,000	72.1	2152	913	27.4
35,000	63.1	1883	827	28.4
30,000	54.1	1614	741	29.6
25,000	45.1	1346	655	31.4
20,000	36.0	1074	568	34.1
15,000	27.0	805	482	38.6
10,000*	18.0	537	396	47.5
5,000*	9.0	268	241	57.8

* SPECIAL MINIMUM BENEFIT RULES MAY APPLY AT THIS LEVEL TO INCREASE THE PIA ABOVE THAT SHOWN HERE.

EXAMPLE

Assume that you reached 62 years of age in 1992 and had an income of $30,000 that year and had a very long history of paying Social Security tax at levels below the maximum. This income is 54.1% of the maximum taxable income of $55,500. Your AIME would then be 54.1% of $2985 or $1,615. The PIA on this amount would be $741 a month. (Table 3, Appendix B-2 gives a more detailed listing of PIAs for various values of AIME.) If you were to retire this year at age 62, your benefits would be 80% of this or $592 a month. If you were to wait three years to retire at age 65, you would have no reduction and the benefit would be increased by the cost of living in the three years between age 62 and 65. Assuming a 4% per year inflation, the monthly benefit would be about 12% higher or $830 a month.

COST OF LIVING INCREASES (COLA)

Social Security insurance benefits are normally adjusted each year for inflation. The following table (7-4) gives the cost of living increases in the PIA for the last 16 years. No year has been skipped, although in 1983 it was delayed for six months.

TABLE 7-4

DATE	PERCENT INCREASE	DATE	PERCENT INCREASE
6/76	6.4	12/84	3.5
6/77	5.9	12/85	3.1
6/78	6.5	12/86	1.3
6/79	9.9	12/87	4.2
6/80	14.3	12/88	4.0
6/81	11.2	12/89	4.7
6/82	7.4	12/90	5.4
12/83	3.5	12/91	3.7
1976-1991 AVERAGE		5.9	
1982-1991 AVERAGE		4.1	

The increases are set in December of a given year but payable beginning in January of the next year.

CHANGES IN BENEFIT DUE TO
EARLY RETIREMENT

Since drawing benefits earlier than the normal 65 retirement age means you will receive more benefit checks and pay less into the Social Security fund, a reduction in benefit will be made. This reduction is permanent. For example, at age 62, you will get 80% of your full benefit. This reduction will continue as long as you draw benefits. The only exception will be if you stop benefits and work for a period before again drawing benefits.

Workers at 62 years of age or above can draw benefits reduced by 5/9 of 1% for each month under 65 years of age. This translates to the following:

AGE AT RETIREMENT	PERCENT OF PIA
62.0	80.00
62.5	83.33
63.0	86.67
63.5	90.00
64.0	93.33
64.5	96.67
65.0	100.00

Legislation passed in 1983 increases the normal retirement age from 65 to 67. This increase is gradual beginning in the year 2003 and slowly increasing to the year 2027. Because of this, reductions in benefits at age 62 will slowly lower from 80% of the PIA to 70% over this same period.

INCREASE IN BENEFIT DUE TO
LATE RETIREMENT

If you do not draw benefits immediately on reaching age 65, you will receive an increased benefit up to age 70. The increases are going through a period of transition. The actual amount of increase depends on your year of birth.

YEAR OF BIRTH	INCREASE PER YEAR DELAY
1917-24	3.0%
1925-26	3.5%
1927-28	4.0%
1929-30	4.5%
1931-32	5.0%
1933-34	5.5%
1935-36	6.0%
1937-38	6.5%
1939-40	7.0%
1941-42	7.5%
1943 UP	8.0%

SPECIAL MINIMUM BENEFIT

A special situation has been recognized where a worker has a long history of earnings but at a low level. The benefits depend upon the number of years of significant coverage as defined below:

YEARS	CALCULATION OF YEARS
1937 TO 1950	Total divided by $900 to get Maximum of 14 years
1951 TO 1978	Must have 25% of maximum taxed amount for each year of credit.
1979 to 1990	Must have about 19% of maximum taxable for each year of credit.
1990 TO DATE	Must have about 11% of maximum taxable for each year of credit.

Based on these credits you would be eligible for a monthly amount equal to $23.90 a month for each year of credit above a minimum of ten and to a maximum of 30. Thus, in 1992 the minimum is $23.90 per month for 11 years of credit to a maximum of $478.20 a month for 30 years of credit.

You have the option of using this special minimum benefit or the regularly calculated benefit, whichever gives you a higher figure.

FAMILY BENEFITS

Your spouse and children may also be eligible for benefits based on your retirement figure. The following table gives the amounts your spouse and child would receive at your retirement and if you are receiving benefits.

DEPENDENT	PERCENT OF YOUR PIA
Spouse below age 62	none
Spouse at age 62	37.5%
Spouse at age 65	50%
Spouse any age with eligible child under age 16	50%
Each eligible child	50%

Note 1.   The increase for age is evenly spread over the 62 to 65 years of age.

Note 2   An eligible child is any unmarried child under 18 or 19 if still in high school. Disabled children of any age who were disabled before age 22.

Note 3.   These are subject to a maximum family benefit of 188% of your PIA.

Note 4.   Payments to the child stop when he/she reaches 18 years of age or marries. Payments to the spouse stop when the child reaches age 16.

DIVORCED SPOUSE

A divorced spouse receives the same benefits as the spouse. There are a few special rules here.

The divorced spouse must have been married to the insured for at least 10 years.

The insured worker must be at least 62 years of age.

The benefits are not dependent on the insured spouse drawing benefits, but if the insured spouse is still working after 62 years of age, the divorce must have existed for at least two years.

The divorced spouse can start at age 62 with the same reduction in benefits as a normal spouse.

If the divorced spouse has remarried, the new insured spouse would generally be the basis for benefits and would follow the rules given in the previous section.

If the divorced spouse marries a person receiving benefits as a dependent, the divorced spouse may still be eligible for benefits based on the work history of the original spouse.

EARNINGS WHILE DRAWING

SOCIAL SECURITY BENEFITS

You may still have some earned income without penalty as follows:

Your Age	1992 Limit w/o penalty
Between 62 and 65	$ 7,440
Between 65 and 69	$10,200
Above 70	No Limit

The limits are revised each year to reflect average increases in earnings.

Under 65 years of age each two dollars earned above the limit will lower your benefits by one dollar. Between 65 and 69 each three dollars you earn above the limit will lower your benefits by one dollar.

Earnings may be considered those from "sweat." Most earnings such as interest, dividends, pensions, trust income, annuity income, etc. are not counted as earnings.

If you start retirement benefits in the middle of a year after having drawn income the first portion of the year, this income is not counted as earnings after starting benefits and will not reduce your benefit that year.

MILITARY SERVICE

Since 1957 military personnel have paid Social Security taxes under certain rules. Before this date (1940 to 1956), military service is credited at $160 per month of service provided you are not receiving a military pension for these same years. These credits are not shown on your record of earnings and should be added at the time of starting to draw benefits.

OTHER RULES

There are many rules and regulations covering many special situations. These include reductions for military or railroad pensions, and other deviations due to disability or care of other dependents. You should check with the

Social Security Administration for these
special situations.

B. DISABILITY BENEFITS

The main concern of this book is for
retirement, but since disability could be
a factor, this brief summary is included.
This should not be considered the final
word on disability benefits. It is a
very complicated subject and will require
rulings from the Social Security
Administration for resolution.

ELIGIBILITY

If you become disabled to the point
that you are not expected to be able to
work for the next 12 months or the
illness could result in early death, you
may be eligible for disability benefits.
Benefits do not begin until five months
after the disability begins.

To be eligible, medical doctors must
certify the injury or illness and you
must have the required quarters of
coverages given by the following table
for 1992:

YEAR OF BIRTH	QUARTERS	YEAR OF BIRTH	QUARTERS
1926	37	1942	27
1927	38	1943	26
1928	39	1944	25
1929	40	1945	24
1930	39	1946	23
1931	38	1947	22
1932	37	1948	21
1933	36	1949-1960	20
1934	35	1961	19
1935	34	1962	17
1936	33	1963	15
1937	32	1964	13
1938	31	1965	11
1939	30	1966	9
1940	29	1967	7
1941	28	1967	6

In the above years of birth, 20 of the quarters must have been earned in the last 10 years. In the following years (1961 and later), the quarters of coverage must be after age 21. The quarters for 1967 must be in the last three years.

CALCULATION OF BENEFIT AMOUNT

Appendix D-2 covers the rigorous calculation of disability benefits. The calculation is similiar to that for retirement benefits.

Your benefit is equal to your PIA at the time the disability occurred. It is not reduced for age unless you had started receiving retirement benefits at age 62. In this case the benefit will be reduced to take into account the time you received retirement benefits.

In no case is the disability PIA
less than that for retirement. It may be
higher because fewer years of earnings
are required in the AIME calculation.
Thus, your benefits are equal to your
PIA. See Appendix D-2.

MAXIMUM FAMILY BENEFIT

The PIA is the amount the wage
earner will receive regardless of age.
This is one major difference from
retirement benefits. The spouse and
eligible children benefits are the same
as if you had retirement benefits. The
maximum family benefit is 150% of the PIA
or 85% of AIME but never less than the
PIA. The maximum is 150% of your PIA.

RESTRICTIONS AND SPECIAL RULES

Disability benefits are not approved
for life but periodically must be
recertified. If you can do other
substantial work (i.e. $500 per month)
you may be disallowed benefits.

There are separate rules for
blindness. For example $810 per month is
the level of substantial work. There are
other differences that can be explained
better by the Social Security
Administration.

There is a trial work period allowed
while you receive disability benefits to
see if you can be gainfully employed.
This trial period is nine months (not
necessarily consecutive months) in which

you may continue to receive benefits and earn money.

Another benefit for some types of disabilities is a rehabilitation program. Services such as counseling and training may be provided if it is believed such services could return you to productivity.

After you have been disabled for 24 months you become eligible for Medicare benefits.

If you are dissatisfied by the outcome of your request for benefits, the decision may be appealed, particularly if you have further information. You can even appeal again to a higher level. The odds are not good for reversal of any decision.

C. SURVIVOR BENEFITS

The death of a fully insured or currently insured worker may lead to benefits for his/her survivors. This is a less well known aspect of the Social Security system and may have considerable value to you by allowing you to reduce or eliminate the life insurance you carry.

ELIGIBILITY FOR

SURVIVOR BENEFITS

Surviving heirs may be eligible for benefits after your death if you are either currently insured or fully insured. To be fully insured you must have worked the required minimum quarters of coverage as given in the following table. If you are near retirement age, these are the same number of quarters required to be eligible for retirement benefits. If you have earned at least six quarters of coverage in the last 13 consecutive calendar quarters you will be currently insured.

QUARTERS TO BE FULLY INSURED

YEAR OF BIRTH	QUARTER	YEAR OF BIRTH	QUARTER
1924	35	1944	25
1925	36	1945	24
1926	37	1946	23
1927	38	1947	22
1928	39	1948	21
1929	40	1949	20
1930	39	1950	19
1931	38	1951	18
1932	37	1952	17
1933	36	1953	16
1934	35	1954	15
1935	34	1955	14
1936	33	1956	13
1937	32	1957	12
1938	31	1958	11
1939	30	1959	10
1940	29	1960	9
1941	28	1961	8
1942	27	1962	7
1943	26	1962	6

WHO RECEIVES THE BENEFIT
(Fully Insured)

The following table lists the amounts your heirs may be eligible to receive:

```
Spouse 65 or over          100.0% of PIA
Spouse 62 or over           82.9% of PIA
Spouse 60 or over           71.5% of PIA
Spouse 50-59 Disabled       71.5% of PIA
Spouse under 61 with
   eligible child           75.0% of PIA
Each child                  75.0% of PIA
```

Children receive benefits up to age 18. The spouse caring for a child under 18 will receive the benefits only until the child is 16 years of age.

A divorced spouse is eligible for the same benefits as the spouse if the marriage lasted at least 10 years. This includes children of the insured who are living with the divorced spouse.

WHO RECEIVES THE BENEFIT
(Currently Insured)

Heirs of a "Currently Insured" worker receive lower benefits than heirs of a fully insured worker. A spouse caring for an eligible child who is under 16 or disabled before age 22 receives benefits as a percentage of PIA as given above.

An eligible child under age 18, 19 if in school, or a child disabled before age 22, receives benefits as a percentage of PIA as given above.

The lump sum benefit is payable with the restrictions as given above.

CALCULATION OF AMOUNT OF BENEFIT

The calculation for the amount of benefits are very similar to those of retirement and disability benefits. The rigorous calculations are described in Appendix D-2.

MAXIMUM FAMILY BENEFIT

The maximum family benefit in 1992 is 150% of the first $495 of your PIA, plus 272% of the next $219, plus 134% of the next $217, plus 175% of the excess of $931. This puts the range between 150% to 187.4% of the PIA.

The benefits received by a divorced spouse do not influence this maximum family benefit unless the divorced spouse is caring for a child of the insured. This is then included in the Maximum Family Benefit.

LUMP-SUM DEATH BENEFIT

If you are working or retired and die, a lump-sum of $255 is paid to your spouse who is living with you at death. If there is no spouse, it is payable to heirs who are eligible for monthly payments at your death. If there are no eligible heirs, there is no payment.

CHAPTER 8

MEDICAL INSURANCE
MEDICAL COSTS

Medical costs are the fastest rising component of our cost of living. These costs could be a significant part of your cost of retirement. As people get older, medical care becomes more important since we seem to have more ailments than our younger friends. A retired person should not be without medical insurance unless they are very wealthy. Without adequate medical insurance, a lengthy illness or hospital stay could wipe out your life savings.

The object of this section is to give you some insight into what your costs will be after retirement and to point out the factors that may be important to you.

Since Medicare insurance is available only after age 65, you will require private insurance before that age. In addition, you may feel you need private medical insurance (Medigap) to supplement Medicare after you are age 65.

A. PRIVATELY INSURED MEDICAL PLANS

Since medical costs are potentially a large retirement cost, it is essential that you understand your current policy, whether acquired on your own or supplied by your work place when you retire. You should also understand the coverage by Medicare, and the possible need for a Medicare supplemented insurance policy.

MEDICAL INSURANCE AFTER RETIREMENT

If you are contemplating retirement, one of your first orders of business must be to study the medical plan you will have after retirement. Many companies have very extensive plans, where your cost is very little and pays good benefits. Other plans have good benefits but your payments may be modest, or high. All will require that at age 65 you subscribe to both Part A and Part B of medicare.

You must start with an evaluation of your employer's insurance which may be available to you. If it is a group plan and if the employer is paying any part of it, it probably will be cheaper than any other type of private plan. Some questions you should be able to answer about your plan are:

1. What benefits will I receive?
2. Is my family covered under these benefits?
3. What percentage of the insurance cost must I bear?

4. Does my share of the cost remain constant or will it change?
5. Does the company have the right to change the benefits or cost to me after I retire?
6. Is the offer of medical benefits to you in writing?
7. How long will the benefits continue?
8. What happens to my spouse's benefits and other dependent's benefits at my death?
9. Do I have to take both parts of Medicare (A and B) when I become eligible?
10. What happens to the benefits if I take another job that has benefits?
11. What happens if I retire from a second job that does not have retirement benefits?
12. What happens to my benefits if the company goes bankrupt or cannot pay? How secure is my company now?
13. What is the amount of maximum extended coverage?
14. How does the policy cover a catastrophic illness?

You must remember, by law an employer must offer its health insurance to a departing employee for an 18-month period (36 months for a child or separated spouse.) They can charge their costs plus a small fee. Find out what this insurance would cost you.

You must be certain who is covered under your plan. Since most plans require you to subscribe to Medicare when you become 65 years of age, and since Medicare is an individual coverage, you could find your spouse and dependents without coverage. You must learn what coverage your spouse and dependents have

under the group plan. Your spouse and
other dependents may have many years
until they are eligible for medicare.

One pitfall of the corporate promise
is the tendency of some companies to
renege on their promises or go bankrupt.
There are several cases in the courts now
where individuals or groups of
individuals are suing corporations for
failing to hold to what the employee
thought was a "good faith" promise. In
some of these cases the medical insurance
was offered as an incentive to take early
retirement.

The apparent legal position is
unless the company made specific promises
(in writing), they can let the retiree
pay more of the heath insurance bill.
Often a company will offer a specific
health plan as part of a retirement
incentive package. Here, the company is
liable in the eyes of the court.

Almost all medical insurance is
cheaper under a group plan than an
individual buying it alone. A major
pitfall of individual insurance is the
tendency of the insurer to raise rates
after a claim to the point that you
switch carriers. Insurance companies
would like to insure only those who have
few claims. Group policies spread the
costs of the high risk person over the
claims of many people.

If you find you have some form of
medical and hospitalization plan provided
by your company, this probably will be a
core plan for you, since the company
probably pays at least some portion of
the cost. You may want to add to that

plan or supplement it with another plan. There are many types of groups offering some form of medical and hospitalization insurance. Typical of groups are AARP, the college of which you may be an alumnus, and trade groups such as The American Chemical Society. Concerns such as Blue Cross/Blue Shield claim to have plans for individuals, but with costs similar to group plans. My experience with AARP is that they endorse such a hodge-podge of medical plans it is hard to tell what is good or bad.

INSURANCE COST FACTORS

As with other insurance, the cost of medical insurance will depend on several factors. Some of these are:

1. Your age and the ages of others insured under the policy.
2. The type of coverage you have.
3. The deductible level that you must pay before receiving benefits for a claim.
4. Whether the policy is a group or individual plan.
5. The carrier.
6. The geographical area in which you live.
7. Your health at the time you take out the insurance. Some illnesses may mean you cannot get the insurance or that claims on it will not be honored.
8. Your status as a smoker or non-smoker may raise or lower rates.

All policies should be expected to cover at least most hospital and medical doctor charges (less the deductible portion). Most do not cover nursing home charges unless they are part of a recovery from a hospital stay.

In purchasing your medical insurance you must decide what you feel should be covered. If you have a pre-existing condition, be careful because it could be totally excluded. If you use chiropractors, for example, they also may be excluded. If you must purchase medical and hospitalization insurance, I suggest that you get proposals from several insurers and that you compare all the provisions and the costs. Make sure the insurer is rated A+ by A.M. Best Company (An insurance company rating service) and by at least one other rating service. Lately, even these ratings may not be adequate. Today many companies are on the verge of bankruptcy, so serious efforts must be devoted to finding the solid company that will, in fact, pay your claims. A good place to start for comparative prices is Blue Cross/Blue Shield.

EXAMPLES OF MEDICAL

INSURANCE POLICIES

A typical policy is described below to give you some ideas of rates and coverages you might expect. This policy is presented for information only and may not be the best you could get. These were quarterly rates, good through December 31, 1991. (Age 65 and over are

with Parts A and B of Medicare). These
rates excluded some large metropolitan
areas.

	SMOKER		NON-SMOKER	
AGE	MALE	FEMALE	MALE	FEMALE
$250 DEDUCTIBLE				
60-64	969.79	1,260.77	872.89	1,134.81
65 & OVER	356.83	463.88	321.18	417.53
$500 DEDUCTIBLE				
60-64	916.74	1,207.73	825.15	1,087.06
65 & OVER	303.78	410.83	273.43	369.78
$1,000 DEDUCTIBLE				
60-64	810.61	1,101.60	729.62	991.54
65 & OVER	207.88	304.70	187.11	274.26
$2,500 DEDUCTIBLE				
60-64	492.30	783.25	443.11	705.00
65 & OVER	136.54	177.47	122.90	159.74

The category for age 65 and over
will be equivalent to what is called
Medigap insurance. Note the rates are
much lower than the next younger age
category. The government carries 60 to
75% of the cost if you are over 65. The
section on Medigap Insurance gives costs
of another specific Medicare Supplement
policy.

You will note the significant
differences for age, sex, and smoking
status. This policy covers hospital and
medical expenses prescribed by a
physician up to the deductibility limit.

    A.   Hospital charges (semi-private
       room) and related expenses.
    B.   Doctor charges.
    C.   Diagnostic expenses.

D.   Physiotherapy charges.
E.   Ambulance (Up to $50).
F.   Blood, blood plasma.
G.   Prescription drugs in hospital or convalescent home.
H.   Artificial limbs, etc.
I.   Hospice service up to 210 days.
J.   Birthing center charges.
K.   Convalescent home for up to 50 days.
L.   Oxygen and anesthetics charges.
M.   Home health care up to 50 days.
N.   Foot surgery.
O.   Limited benefits up to dollar maximums on psychiatric and private duty nursing.

Items not covered include:
A.   Any expenses for a pre-existing condition, unless at least 12 months have passed without any type of treatment or medication for the illness.
B.   Routine physical examinations (Some exceptions).
C.   Outpatient prescription drugs.
D.   Several other items.

For some people, the cost of outpatient drugs may be a major cost amounting to several thousands of dollars per year. Neither this policy nor the one described under Medigap Insurance covers this.

B. MEDICARE

A major benefit to you of the Social Security system is the Medicare program. Medicare provides both hospital and medical benefits. The hospital benefit portion (Part A) is without extra cost while the medical portion (Part B) requires a monthly payment. These benefits are available only if you are at least 65 years old. A supplemental insurance plan is required to cover costs that Medicare does not cover.

WHO IS COVERED

- If you are 65 and receiving retirement benefits, or are eligible for retirement benefits you are eligible for Medicare. It is not a family plan. Only the individual is covered.
- If you have been disabled and entitled to disability benefits for 24 months under Social Security, you are entitled to Medicare benefits.
- If you or your dependent suffers chronic kidney failure that requires dialysis or kidney transplant, and if you have been insured by Social Security on your job, you are eligible for Medicare.

There are several caveats that come into play, of which you should become aware:

- Only an individual is covered, not the family.
- You must be 65 to be eligible. Your spouse is only eligible when he/she is also 65.
- You can apply for Medicare without taking retirement benefits.
- If you are not insured by the Social Security system you can buy the medicare benefits by paying for both the part A and Part B sections.   In 1991 the cost of Part A was $177.00

per month and Part B was $31.80 per month in 1992.
- There are enrollment times each year when you can apply for Medicare.
- If you delay subscribing to Part B past age 65, the cost will increase by 10% for each year of delay.
- Extended nursing home care is covered only under very unusual circumstances. Do not count on Medicare to cover this item.
- Part B premiums are escalated each year based on the previous year's increase in medical costs. The 1992 cost was $31.80 per month. A $100 annual deductible was also in effect in 1992.
- Part B premiums cover only about 25% of the medical costs. The balance comes from the U.S Government's general income. Thus, if you are in average health, it is well worth the price.

MEDICARE COVERED PARTS A AND B

The Medicare program covers about one-half of the average cost of individual medical expenses. It is not designed to cover all costs to you.

A full description of the benefits is well beyond the scope of this section. You should get more detailed information from the Social Security Administration.

PART A   (1992 COVERAGES AND COSTS)

HOSPITAL COVERAGE
Medical Services Covered   Your Cost
Days 1-60 $652 One time deductible
Days 61-90 $163 per day co-insurance
Lifetime reserve days $326 per day co-insurance
   (60 per lifetime)
SKILLED NURSING CARE FACILITY
Days 1-20   No charge
Days 21-100 $81.50 per day co-insurance
HOME HEALTH CARE   No charge

The reimbursements are per benefit period. A benefit period is one illness unless there are 60 days between hospital or skilled care facility stays. The skilled care facility requires that you have been in a hospital and have a doctor's certificate requiring the special care. The reimbursements in the hospital and skilled care facility cover the normal expenses for such a facility, but do not cover:

> Private rooms
> Private duty nurses
> Personal comfort items such as telephone, T.V. Doctor services which are covered under Part B.

PART B

This part covers the medical portion of Medicare. This includes physicians' fees, both for hospital confinement and for office visits and outpatient services such as physical therapy. It covers laboratory services, X-rays, prosthetic devices and similar services. It does not cover routine physicals,

immunizations, hearing aids, eyeglasses
nor prescription drugs.

MEDIGAP INSURANCE

Because of the large deductibles of
hospitalization coverage, the short
covered confinement periods, and the lack
of coverage for prescription drugs, most
people find it necessary to supplement
Medicare with additional medical
insurance. This coverage is offered by
many companies but at wide variation in
costs and benefits. This type of
coverage may vary in cost from $50 to 100
per month up to several thousand dollars
per year. All the policies have an
escalation with age. As you get older,
the cost will increase.

Because of the confusion with these
policies and because of the tendency of
Senior Citizens to buy unneeded coverage,
the thousands of types of policies will
soon be covered by ten different policies
that will have standard benefits. The ten
policies will all include a core of
services with extras possible for skilled
nursing home, hospital deductible, doctor
deductible, excess doctor charges,
foreign travel, at home recovery,
prescription drugs and preventive
screening. It may be another two years
before these plans will be in effect. It
is very doubtful if all coverages would
be required for a person.

Another example of a Medicare
supplemented insurance policy is given
below with individual costs ranging from
$560 to $1,550 per year. This policy
will cover the deductible and co-

insurance exclusions from Medicare Part A
and the 20% co-insurance of Part B. It
has a $100 deductible. The monthly costs
of this policy in 1991 are as follows:

MONTHLY PAYMENTS FOR MEDIGAP INSURANCE

ENROLLMENT AGE	POLICY 1	POLICY 2	POLICY 3
65	$46.50	$56.30	$69.00
66-69	54.10	68.50	81.70
70-74	67.40	91.20	103.90
75-79	72.30	103.10	115.80
80 +	77.10	114.60	127.40

Policies 1 and 2 cover the
deductible and co-insurance requirements
of Part A and the 20% co-insurance of
Part B except, $100 deductible. They
also cover most out-of-country
emergencies. The extra cost of Policy 3
covers automatic claims filing. Policy 1
does not cover the $628 deductible nor
the $157 per day charge for days 101 to
365 in a skilled nursing care facility
while recuperating.

MEDICAID

Medicaid is a form of medical
insurance mandated by the Federal
Government but administered and paid for
by the states, with some federal subsidy.
This medical coverage is available to all
families with very low income and few
assets. The rules vary from state to
state, but most require the family assets
to be dissipated before a spouse becomes
eligible for Medicaid. Assets (except
for a home, in some states) must either
be spent or given away 24 to 30 months

before becoming eligible for Medicaid.

Books are available that describe the legal path to be followed, to avoid the bankrupting cost of long term nursing care. For many people the psychological costs of poverty to become eligible for Medicaid need may be too large to accept.

C. NATIONAL MEDICAL COSTS

The Bureau of Labor Statistics measures the total medical costs in the United States. These data are used in the tables of this section: The medical costs for the past several years are as follows:

YEAR	1970	1980	1985	1987
TOTAL (BILLION $)	75	248	419	500
ANNUAL % CHANGE	12.3	12.7	7.9	9.8
PER CAPITA ($)	349	1055	1696	1987
% GNP	7	9	10	11
% PRIVATE	63	58	58	59
% PUBLIC	37	42	42	41
PRIVATE EXPENDITURES				
TOTAL (BILLION $)	47	143	244	293
DIRECT PAY %	56	44	42	40
INSUR. PREMIUM %	36	51	53	54
OTHER %	8	5	5	4
PUBLIC EXPENDITURES				
TOTAL (BILLION $)	28	105	175	207
MEDICARE %	27	35	41	40
MEDICAID %	23	27	25	26
DEFENSE/VET %	13	10	9	9
OTHER %	37	28	25	25

The category "other" includes research, education, safety and OSHA.

Some significant points of these data are:

1. The total expenditures are rising very rapidly.
2. The total fraction the government supplies has quit rising so that the increases are now shared equally between private and public expenditure.
3. The percentage of public expenditure going to medicare appears to have leveled off after rapid increases.
4. The private sector fraction going to health insurance premiums is still increasing.

This says you as a retired individual will be paying more for your health insurance, unless you have a very exceptional heath care policy paid for by your former employer.

The annual cost to the consumer for medical care has been developed by age group as follows:

ANNUAL CONSUMER UNIT EXPENDITURES
FOR HEALTH CARE 1987

| AGE | AMOUNT | PERCENTAGE OF TOTAL | | |
		HEALTH INSUR.	MEDICAL SERVICES	DRUGS & SUPPLIES
UNDER 25	$ 338	29.3%	45.9%	24.9%
25 - 34	766	32.2	46.6	21.1
35 - 44	1085	29.8	49.9	20.4
45 - 54	1255	30.5	44.9	24.6
55 - 65	1383	34.6	38.5	26.8
65 - 74	1688	39.6	34.7	25.8
75 & OVER	1596	43.0	28.1	28.9
ALL UNITS	1135	34.5	41.1	24.3

For the above 65 age groups the health care costs are even larger since most of the Medicare and a significant part of Medicaid goes to this group of people. The drop for the above 75 age group in total expenditure is probably influenced by the lower income of this group.

D. SUMMARY OF MEDICAL COSTS

The table given below summarizes 1992 medical costs that are generally applicable. Your situations may be slightly different. The main variables are: 1. Age, since you must subscribe to Medicare at age 65, and 2. How much of your medical bill your former employer pays. The individual costs in the table are those medical costs you must pay outside of your policies. They include deductibles and items not covered.

MEDICAL COSTS 1992
ANNUAL COSTS PER PERSON

RETIREE - AGES 55 TO 65

	MINIMUM	MAXIMUM
INDIVIDUAL COSTS	$ 500	$1,500
RETIREE PAID INS.	2,000	4,000
TOTAL	$2,500	$5,500
INDIVIDUAL COSTS	$ 500	$1,500
EMPLOYER PAID INS.	$ 0	3,000
TOTAL	$ 500	$4,500

RETIREE - AGES 65 AND UP

	MINIMUM	MAXIMUM
INDIVIDUAL COSTS	$1,000	$2,500
MEDICARE	382	382
RETIREE PAID INS.	550	1,800
TOTAL	$1,932	$4,682
INDIVIDUAL COSTS	$1,000	$2,500
MEDICARE	382	382
EMPLOYER PAID INS.	0	1,500
TOTAL	$1,382	$4,382

A sad part of the medical insurance picture is the increases in costs of 10% per year that have existed for the last 10 to 15 years, and are projected for the next few years. The U.S. Commerce Department, in December, 1991 predicted that overall medical costs will increase by 12 to 13% per year over the next five years. This type of increase could easily bring medical insurance costs to be the largest item in our budgets. Increases of this magnitude will double the cost every seven years. A modest $3,000 medical insurance bill today could become $12,000 in 20 years.

CHAPTER 9

INSURANCE

Insurance is a major item in everyone's budget. Between life, property, automobile and medical insurance, the costs can easily amount to many thousands of dollars per year. Some people have even other kinds of insurance. I remember that Betty Grable insured her legs. This section is to suggest means for reducing the amounts paid for some types of insurance.

Insurance provides protection for losses you cannot afford to absorb. You are betting the Insurance Company that something will happen to cause you a loss. The Insurance Company is betting that this loss will not occur or that if it does occur, it will be less than expected. When you take out insurance, the Insurance Company has made a "Risk-Benefit Analysis" that tells them the benefit to insuring you is greater than the risk.

Insurance companies must make a profit to stay in business. They also have substantial expenses in maintaining the organization necessary to service its patrons. The sales people that sell insurance make commissions on the sales as their livelihood. Thus, much of the premium you pay for the insurance is for overhead, with only a portion of the premium set aside to pay for losses. Only 40 to 60% of premiums are paid out in claims.

Besides minor cost saving possibilities, the only way to save significantly on insurance costs is to take a greater portion of the risk yourself. Retirement is a time you may want to absorb more of your risks since you may have greater cash available to you to do so.

The increased need and cost of medical insurance counters the potential lower cost of property and life insurance. Medical costs are discussed in Chapter 8.

The most common types of property insurance are automobile and housing insurance. Both are necessary but both may be candidates for lower premiums. Both have premium costs that can vary with geographical location and other factors.

AUTOMOBILE INSURANCE

Automobile insurance has three basic parts -- liability, collision and comprehensive. By law, liability insurance is required and seems prudent to have in our litigious society where lawyers advertise on television for clients.

Collision and comprehensive insurance are another story and are candidates for lower premiums. Collision insurance covers damage to your car caused by a moving vehicle. Comprehensive insurance covers damage by other than collision. Collision generally has a deductible amount you must pay before you receive benefits from the insurer while comprehensive insurance may not have a deductible minimum. The cost of collision insurance is almost independent of the age of the automobile or its value since it costs about as much to fix an old car as it does a new car.

COST FACTORS

AUTOMOBILE INSURANCE

Automobile insurance premiums are influenced by a variety of factors. The following list gives ideas on where to look to reduce automobile premiums. Most of the time you have to ask for the discounts.

1. Type of automobile.
2. Number of drivers for an automobile.
3. Age of the drivers.
4. The city or location in which you live. Rates vary considerably by location.
5. Use of the automobile. Rates vary according to whether the automobile is driven to the place of employment each day. At retirement there is generally a break here for you.
6. The level of deductible you maintain. The higher the deductible the lower the premium.

7. Differences in rates between companies. Get competitive bids.
8. Many states use a traffic ticket point system that can drastically increase rates if you receive tickets.
9. Multiple automobiles on one policy can give a discount on rates. Rates also may be lower if you have both automobile and home insurance with the same company.
10. Incidental items. Towing and medical insurance can add to the bill.

Collision insurance covers damage to the automobile. It is limited to the value of the automobile less the deductible amount. If an old car is damaged beyond repair you will only receive the value of the old car. They will not pay for repairs if the cost is higher than the blue book value of the automobile.

Some states may have no fault insurance in which the insurer pays regardless of fault. Many people have serious complaints with insurance companies after settlement of collision accident claims when they are left with remaining car payments and no car. Automobiles with four and five year notes, are at times worth less than the amount owed. Insurers cover only up to the value of the automobile as seen through their eyes not yours.

COST REDUCTION OPPORTUNITIES

If you have a new $30,000 automobile, the $150-500/year premium for collision insurance with a $250 deduction may not seem excessive. However, if your automobile is several years old and valued at $3,000, and your premium is $300/year with the same $250 deduction, you may consider dropping the collision insurance. In making these decisions, you should consider your accident record. Two accidents in the last 40 years would lead you to believe you are not accident prone, but if you have had two accidents in the last five years you may be at risk. Your age, eyesight and general health may influence your consideration of this point.

The variation in premiums (1991) that I found on my two automobiles were as follows:

Deductible	$250	$500	$1,000
Liability	535	535	535
Comprehensive	156	156	156
Collision	294	226	192
Other items	78	78	78
Total	$1,065	$995	$961

Remember that the limit of the property damage to your car is the book value of the car. Using the above cases, a savings of $70 increases your risk to loss by $250 and a savings of $102 increases your risk by $750. You may consider these savings insignificant. If your car is only worth $3000 the savings in collision and comprehensive insurance costs of $348 to 450 may be important.

HOME INSURANCE

Home insurance is probably necessary because most people have a very large investment in their home. The deductible is again a fertile region to look for savings. My advice here is to take the largest deductible you feel you can afford.

What you really need is catastrophic coverage if a fire or other event totally destroys a home. Significant savings may be possible with deductible levels of $1000 to $5000.

I received quotations (1991 dollars) on two different homes with two levels of deductions.

Deductible	$500	$1000
Home No 1	$780	$582
Home No 2	471	373

Other factors that may lower your home insurance include a senior citizen discount and bringing the plumbing and electrical systems up to the standards of almost new homes. I saved a significant sum with these two items. Many companies give a break if you have smoke alarms, fire extinguishers, or dead bolt locks on outside doors. You have to ask for these savings.

SELF INSURANCE OR CO-INSURANCE

Let's assume, between automobile and your home, you increase your financial exposure to reduce your premium costs by $500 per year. You would like to know how much you should have available to cover emergencies. Assume you increase your risk by $5000 to save $500 per year. Assume that once every 10 years you would spend an extra $1000 and once every 20 years you would spend an extra $5000. These are random events and cannot be predicted but assume the $1000 losses occur after 5 and 15 years and the $5000 loss occurs after 10 years.

If you set aside $2000 in a special account for the major emergency and put in $500 each year for the premium you save, you can set up a table as below. Take 8% interest on the money invested.

TABLE 9-1

SELF INSURANCE FOR COLLISION AND COMPREHENSIVE PORTION OF INSURANCE

	INITIAL INPUT			$2000
	PREMIUM PER YEAR			$ 500
	INTEREST RATE			8% PER YEAR

YEAR	AMOUNT	ADD/ DELETE	INTEREST	NEW VALUE
1	$2000	$500	$200	$2700
2	2700	500	256	3456
3	3456	500	316	4272
4	4272	500	382	5154
5	5154	-500	372	5027
6	5027	500	442	5969
7	5969	500	518	6986
8	6986	500	599	8085
9	8085	500	687	9272
10	9272	-4500	382	5154
11	5154	500	452	6106
12	6106	500	528	7134
13	7134	500	611	8245
14	8245	500	700	9445
15	9445	-500	500	9445
16	9445	500	796	10740
17	10740	500	899	12140
18	12140	500	1011	13651
19	13651	500	1132	15283
20	15283	500	1263	17046

This is the type of calculation you can do for your situation that could satisfy you on the possibilities of self insurance.

Some comments from the above calculations are:

1. The total paid into the fund was $12,000 but there is now a residual

value of $15,283 though $7000 was
paid out over the life time.
2. The particular situation could
have handled larger losses. After
the fifth year there was always at
least $5,000 available for losses.
4. You could start with a larger
initial investment that would cover
emergencies anytime and withdraw the
excess of money when you wish.
Declare a dividend to yourself.
5. The money is yours. In effect
you are forming your mini insurance
company.
6. Get as large a deductible on
automobile and home insurance as you
can afford.
7. Depending on your financial
situation you could easily drop
collision insurance on automobiles
for self insurance, particularly on
older cars.
8. An individual does not have the
advantage of diversification that a
large insurance company has so that
there is an inherent risk that two
events could happen at once or that
one could wipe out the fund in the
early years.

LIFE INSURANCE

How much life insurance do you need?
This question has been asked millions of
times over the years. From the Insurance
Companies' stand point it's "All I can
sell you." There is a rational way of
approaching this that will give you the
prudent person's opinion. Then, there is
the other side: "How much can I afford?"

At retirement age _new_ life insurance of any type becomes very expensive.

The discussions here are only on Life Insurance for personal reasons not business nor estate tax coverage.

If you are thinking about retirement there is a sense that you already have enough set aside for your and your spouse's lifetime needs. There may be special situations that require additional aid after your death, beyond that provided by your assets and Social Security.

If you worked for a large corporation, life insurance is normally not provided after retirement. You may find yourself with much less insurance, and often, no insurance. To some extent, the survivor provisions of Social Security will compensate for this, but the amount may be inadequate. If you are thinking of leaving a situation in which you now have life insurance as an employee benefit, it is prudent that you assess your situation.

The basic way to know how much life insurance you need is to develop a schedule on how much your heirs will need and for how long, after your death. It will be assumed that leaving an estate with an excess of cash is not the primary goal, but the goal would be to leave enough for your dependents to survive adequately.

You have already developed an income statement on financial needs after your retirement and you have developed a list of your assets. These can serve as a

basis for your calculations. Estimation
of the amount of life insurance needed
can best be illustrated by example.
Three examples of different situations
are given in Appendix D-3.

CONCLUSIONS

The general conclusions from these
examples is the benefit gained by having
a given amount of life insurance is about
the same as reducing your spending by the
amount of the cost of the insurance. If
you buy the insurance you must reduce
your standard of living by that amount
since the money is not available to you
for other needs.

If you are a couple and your death
occurs earlier than expected, your spouse
would gain if you had the extra
insurance. However, the needs of the
spouse would be less since only one
person is to be supported. Don't forget
that after your death your spouse is
eligible for 100% of your Social Security
benefits. If your Social Security
benefit is $700 per month and your spouse
is 65 years old, the value of this is
equivalent to $125,000 of life insurance.
Countering this could be the loss of your
pension benefits unless you elected to
receive joint lifetime benefits.

CHAPTER 10

TAXES

Taxes play a controlling role in much of what we do. For many people the impact of taxes at retirement will be greater than expected. For some they may play a minor role. All must consider the effect of taxes. You must know the impact of taxes on what you do at retirement.

This chapter is not intended to replace the need for your study of the tax laws or the need for a tax accountant at the time of your retirement. It is intended to present relevant tax information regarding only those items that could affect your decision on whether to retire. The tax laws will clearly have a major impact on how you handle your retirement money.

The tax impact on such things as IRAs, Lump Sum distributions, annuity payments and SEP/KEOGH funds will be discussed here. Other tax related topics such as home sale and taxes on Social Security also will be discussed.

TAX FAVORED RETIREMENT PLANS

The Federal Government has recognized that Social Security is only a supplement to the retirement needs of Americans and has created many types of savings plans in which taxes are deferred until retirement, or until funds are withdrawn for use. Tax deferred means that no tax is paid on the income of a plan until the money is withdrawn, at which time the taxes must be paid. Depending on the plan, the money put in also may be tax exempt. The money normally paid out early for taxes can earn income, so that there is a benefit to your net worth to have your assets in qualified non-taxed plans. The down side is, you must still pay the taxes as you withdraw the money for use. Normally, you will be in a lower tax bracket after you retire so that you can pay less to use the money.

Chapter 11, Section F has an example of the financial benefits of tax deferred savings over normal savings. The length of time in the plan has a big impact on the improvement over normal savings. For the case given, the improvement was 11% after five years, 22% after 10 years, 36% after 15 years and 52% after 20 years. The moral of this story is, we should have started sooner with our IRAs, 401(k)s and Keogh plans.

TYPES OF TAX DEFFERED PLANS

PLAN   DESCRIPTION

IRA   These are tax deferred
                        plans. The contribution
                        may or may not be
                        deductible. The income is
                        tax deferred in all cases.
                        Thus, funds withdrawn may
                        be fully taxable or
                        partially taxable
                        depending on your
                        contribution situation.

401(k),   These are company plans in
                        which a company puts aside
                        money for your benefit.
                        The money put in is
                        generally from your pay
                        check but is not taxed.
                        The company often matches
                        part of your input. There
                        are limits to the amount
                        that may be put into these
                        funds. Tax on the earned
                        income and on the
                        principal is not due until
                        withdrawn. Funds
                        withdrawn may be fully
                        taxable or only partially
                        taxable depending on your
                        contribution situation.

KEOGH or   These are retirement plans
SERP PLANS   for self employed persons.
                        Contributions are
                        generally tax free and the
                        income earned on the fund
                        is tax free until
                        withdrawn. When money is

withdrawn from a Keogh or Serp the funds are generally 100% taxable.

SEP   This is a simplified employee pension plan. You may have contributed alone to the plan or your employer also may have contributed. Both contributions and income are generally tax deferred. Withdrawals are 100% taxable.

COMPANY PLANS   Many Companies have pension plans that have a variety of methods of contributions. Most have some form of company contribution which may or may not be supplemented by employee contributions. Employee contributions may be tax deferred or taxed. The income on these funds is tax deferred. Thus, the withdrawals from these funds may be totally taxed or partially taxed. Depending on the company agreements, funds from these may be as annuity payments or as a lump sum.

ANNUITIES   These are of two general types, employee annuities and commercial annuities. Employee annuities may have contributions made that are tax free or from your taxed funds. Commercial annuities are

generally bought with
money that has already
been taxed and may have an
insurance provision.
Thus, annuity income may
be totally taxed or only
partially taxed.

GENERAL RULES FOR QUALIFIED PLANS

A qualified plan is one that
qualifies for tax deferral under the
IRS's rules. The following are general
statements for which there may be
exceptions for your particular case.

1. A 10% penalty is assessed on the
    amount withdrawn before age 59.5
    years of age. This is besides the
    normal tax on the withdrawal.
    Exceptions to this are: Separation
    from service over 55 years of age,
    disability, or financial hardship.
    Financial hardship means that all
    other avenues to pay have been
    exhausted. If withdrawals before age
    59.5 become possible for you without
    tax penalty, the payments must
    generally be made over your lifetime.

    An exception may be the periodic
    planned payment from certain
    annuities.

2. Withdrawals must start when you reach
    70.5 years of age. This rule applies
    even if you continue to work. If you
    reach 70.5 years of age in a calendar
    year, you must begin receiving
    payments by April 1 of the following
    year. Certain rules exist on how

much you must withdraw each year.
Tax sheltered annuity benefits
accrued before 1987 are exempt from
the rule. The tax penalty for not
drawing out sufficient funds is 50%
of the shortage. Don't let this go
if you are at this age.

3.   Roll over from one qualified plan to
     another is generally possible. If
     the cash passes through your hands
     you must roll over within 60 days.
     These rollovers allow you to retain
     the tax advantaged status of the
     fund. No taxes are due on the amount
     rolled over. The receiving plan is
     an IRA with all the rights,
     privileges and restrictions
     associated with an IRA.

4.   Direct transfers of cash and
     securities from one institution to
     another are simple for IRA, SEP, and
     KEOGH/SERP plans. The receiving
     institution has a standard form that
     you fill out and sign, that they use
     as authorization for the transfer.
     If you set up your plan in an
     institution that had an agreement you
     could not transfer your account, you
     may be forced to remain with that
     institution. Many company exempt
     plans will not transfer funds to
     other institutions so that the
     transfer feature is not available.

5.   A lump sum distribution may be
     eligible for a single, five or ten
     year averaging, if you were born on
     or before December 31, 1935 and have
     been in the plan for five years. You
     must take the entire lump sum with no
     portion rolled over. The rollover is

irrevocable and bars the use of averaging for this lump sum. Lump sums that may be eligible for the one-time tax averaging, are company pension lump sums, Keogh or Serp accounts, or company 401(k) plans. IRAs are not eligible. If the sum is large, the averaging features may have a higher tax rate than the normal income tax.

6. There are penalties for excess withdrawals from qualified plans. A 15% penalty may be assessed on excesses over $750,000 lump sums or $150,000 per year total withdrawals from qualified plans. Several exceptions exist for distributions not counted in the above totals. If you are in this situation you can afford the accountant to help you.

LUMP SUM DISTRIBUTIONS

A lump sum distribution must be your entire share of an IRS approved pension, bonus, or profit-sharing plan. If there is more than one type of pension plan to which you have contributed, you must include in the lump sum the total funds from the different plans.

You have several options for handling these lump sum payments. Your age may mean the averaging option is not available to you. The options are:

1. You may pay ordinary income tax on the sum and use it as you see fit.

2. You may roll over the entire sum to an IRA and pay no immediate tax. As you withdraw funds you will be required to pay taxes. You may keep the fund intact until you are forced to begin withdrawals at age 70.5.

3. You may make a partial roll over and pay tax on only the portion not rolled over. A restriction here is that you must roll over at least one-half of the lump sum.

4. If you were born before December 31, 1935 you may elect to use 10-year or 5-year averaging, provided you meet the other requirements. The pre-1974 accrual can be treated as a capital gain that may give a tax advantage in certain cases. The capital gains feature is being phased out in 1992 for five year averaging.

   This averaging is of benefit only if you need the money for some reason. In addition, you may have more than one lump sum in which a choice of which to average may be to your benefit. If you are considering a one-time averaging, it will be necessary for you to spend time developing the benefits of five-year versus 10-year averaging.

   Stakes and benefits of lump sum distributions can be large, so you should make every effort to understand the pitfalls and opportunities. The information given here may be inadequate for a final decision. You should take your lump sum details to an accountant.

   You may also need to request considerable information directly from your employer or your fund trustee. For instance, your taxed contributions are not counted in the funds to be taxed and certain contributions before certain dates are considered capital gains.

FIVE OR TEN YEAR AVERAGING

To qualify for five or ten year averaging of a lump sum there are several conditions to be met:

1. The lump sum must be eligible.
2. You must have been in the plan at least 5 years.
3. You must have been born before December 31, 1935.
4. Only once per lifetime averaging is allowed, unless you took one before 1987 and were under 59 1/2 years of age at the time.
5. You can elect either 5-year or 10-year averaging whichever is more advantageous to you.
6. The entire sum must be received in one calendar year.
7. A roll over before withdrawing the lump sum will make it ineligible for averaging treatment.

TEN-YEAR AVERAGING

To estimate the tax, you should know how much of the lump sum is tax free, how much is capital gain and how much is to be ordinary income. The taxes are calculated on the 1986 tax rate that had a flat 20% tax on capital gains. This tax table is in Appendix D-4. You can count the capital gain as either ordinary income or as capital depending on which gives you the lowest tax. The procedure is as follows:

1.   Take the sum to be averaged (including capital gains) and divide by 10.
2.   Calculate the tax based on the 1986 tax tables using the single taxpayer table, Appendix C-4.
3.   Multiply this tax by 10 to get the total taxes due. This is the tax due if you decide not to use the capital gains tax for the capital gains portion. If this tax rate is over 20% you will want to proceed with the capital gains calculation since it is a flat 20%.
4.   Calculate the percentage of the lump sum that is not capital gains.
5.   Multiply the taxes calculated in step 3 by the fraction of step 4. This will be the taxes attributable to ordinary income.
6.   Capital gains are calculated by using the fixed tax rate of 20% in effect in 1986.
7.   Add the capital gains tax to the tax of 5 to get the total tax.

If the sum to be averaged is less than $70,000, there is a "minimum distribution allowance" to be deducted from the amount to be averaged. This figure is calculated as follows:

1.   Take 50% of the amount to be averaged but not more than $10,000.
2.   Subtract $20,000 from the amount to be averaged. Take 20% of the difference.

3.   Subtract the figure of 2 above from
     1 above. This is the minimum
     distribution allowance.
4.   Subtract the minimum distribution
     allowance from the sum to be
     averaged. Divide this number by 10
     and add $2300 to get a figure used
     to calculate the tax. This tax must
     then be multiplied by 10 to get the
     tax you owe on the lump sum.

     An obvious step here is to compare
the tax calculated above with the tax
that would result if you took the entire
sum as ordinary income in the year you
receive the lump sum. The reason this may
be beneficial is that the maximum tax
rates have been lowered from 50 to 31%
since 1986.

     The 1986 tax table for single
taxpayers is given in Appendix C-4. A
table giving the taxes for a total lump-
sum is given in Appendix C-5.

IRA DISTRIBUTIONS

     IRA distributions can be set up for
periodic payments or can be withdrawn as
needed. They can be left intact until
withdrawals are forced by age, or they
can be withdrawn before age 59 1/2 with
the 10% penalty.

     The IRAs can be self directed or
they can be managed by "money managers."
They are the most flexible of all
qualified tax deferred plans. You can
readily move from one trustee institution
to another.

The transfer from one institution to another is generally made directly between the institutions. They can be made by rollover. One pitfall here is that only one rollover is permitted each 12 month period. If you inadvertently draw funds from a plan to put into another plan when you have already made a rollover during the year you must pay taxes on the second rollover.

My experience with rollovers is not totally satisfactory. I have experienced loss of interest for two weeks to two months on the amount rolled over. In addition, sale of assets may be done on good investments that do not fit into the new plan's features. Many months may pass before you are earning the same income as before.

DISTRIBUTIONS AFTER
70 1/2 YEARS OF AGE

You must start drawing from your tax deferred accounts by April 1 following the year you reach age 70 1/2. If you do not draw out enough, the Federal Government assesses a 50% penalty on the difference between what was withdrawn and what should have been withdrawn.

The method of calculation depends on your life expectancy and on the amount in your qualified plan. The calculation is repeated each year so that a new figure is used each year.

The life expectancy is a joint life and last survivor figure determined from the table given in Appendix C-2. The other person to be used is the beneficiary listed by law. If you have listed two or more beneficiaries you must take the oldest. You cannot use a second age more than 10 years younger than your age.

Once you have determined the joint life expectancy, you divide the amount in your IRA by this joint life expectancy to get that year's required withdrawal. This must be repeated each year.

The amount in the IRA should be that of the end of the year before the April 1 payment. If this end of year value is not available to you, the previous year's end value may be used for the April withdrawal, with the corrected figure used by the end of the year.

If you have several IRAs, you must calculate each separately and add them together to get the total amount you must withdraw that year. Though you may have many IRAs, the withdrawal can be from all or from only one, with at least the minimum total withdrawn.

If you do not retire until after age 70 1/2, you can delay withdrawals until April 1 of the year after retirement. This does not apply if you own 5% or more of the business from which you retire. Here, you must make withdrawals even if you are still working.

TAXES ON ANNUITIES

Calculations on the taxes for annuities can be complicated or simple depending on the annuity provisions and the dates at which you purchased them. Laws have changed and life expectancy tables have changed from male and female to a unisex table. (Appendix C-3)

Normally you must pay taxes on the interest earned from annuity investments, but taxes are not on that portion attributed to investments with money that has already been taxed. The institution holding the annuity should provide you with most of the information needed to calculate your taxes. This section is provided to help you estimate the taxes you could pay on annuities since this may be a major part of the money you expect to live on after you retire. A full description of tax ramifications on annuities is beyond the scope of this book. For the purposes here, it is assumed that the annuity is qualified for tax deferment.

Restrictions on annuities are the same as for an IRA. The withdrawals before age 59 1/2 are penalized at 10% and withdrawals must begin by age 70 1/2.

Annuities can be either employee or commercial. They differ in some ways but both have the same tax characteristic. Annuities may have a fixed term or they may be for your life or the joint life of you and your beneficiary. The payments may be fixed in amount or they may vary depending on the earnings of the principal. They may have other features such as lump sum payments, provisions for early withdrawal, and minimum amounts to be paid at death. These factors can all affect the taxes you must pay.

The amount you receive may consist of both a return of your payments or payments in your behalf, and interest earned over time on the invested money. Because of this, it is necessary to estimate the amount of payment that will be taxed and the amount that will not be taxed.

You must learn how much taxed money has been put into the annuity. This is, of course, your money or that of an employer contribution that may have been taxed or not taxed. For a commercial annuity that you purchased, this may be simple. For an employee annuity, you may need help from your employer to get the amount of already taxed contributions.

Once you know how much you put into the annuity, you must calculate how much you expect to receive. The number of payments you expect depends on your life expectancy. Sometimes this may be a fixed number given in the annuity contract. If the amount of each payment is fixed, you simply multiply this amount by the number of payments to get the expected amount to be withdrawn. You then get the fraction of taxed income from the ratio of taxed to untaxed funds over the life of the annuity.

TAXES ON COMMERCIAL ANNUITIES

The cost is the sum of all premiums paid with taxed funds. Your employer may have made payments for you on which you paid income tax. From this cost you must deduct any refunded premiums, dividends, or rebates up to the starting date. Premiums for double indemnity, disability payment features, and values of refund features must be deducted. The holder of the annuity can best supply some of these charges.

Payments received before the starting date that are attributable to contributions before August 14, 1982 reduce the cost of the annuity. Any excess above cost is subject to income tax. For investments on or after August 14, 1982, the premature payments are taxable according to the ratio of untaxed to taxed value of the annuity.

If the total investment in the annuity was made before July 1, 1986, you use the male/female life expectancies of Appendix C-3. If any part of your investment was made on or after July 1, 1986, you must use the unisex life expectancy tables. The joint unisex life expectancy table is the same as used for over 70 1/2 age withdrawals and is given in Appendix C-2.

EXAMPLE 1.

Jim is 62 years old and begins to receive payments of $100 per month. The annuity was totally funded before July 1, 1986.

His total cost of the annuity was
$10,000.

From Appendix C-3, Jim's life expectancy
is 16.9 years.

Total expected payments:

16.9 years x 12 mo./yr. x $100/mo.
                                = $20,280

The fraction to be taxed is:

   (20,280 -10,000)/20,280   = 0.5069

The amount taxed each year is:

   12 x $100 x 0.5069   = $609.48/year

EXAMPLE 2

Take the same situation as above, except
some contributions were made after July
1, 1986. Here, the unisex table in
Appendix C-2 gives a life expectancy of
22.5 years.

The expected return is:

    22.5 yr. x 12 mo./yr. x $100/mo.
                             = $27,000

The taxable fraction is:

   (27,000 -10,000)/27,000   = 0.6296

The amount taxed each year is:

   12 mo x $100/mo x 0.6296 = $755.52

        If payments are made quarterly,
semi-annually or annually, an adjustment
must be made in the life expectancy

figures. The adjustment depends on the
months from the annuity starting date to
the date of the first payment as follows:

LIFE EXPECTANCY ADJUSTMENTS

Number of whole months between annuity
starting date and first payment

Months	Quarterly	Semi-Annually	Annually
0 - 1	+0.1	+0.2	+0.5
2	0.0	+0.1	+0.4
3	-0.1	0.0	+0.3
4		0.0	+0.2
5		-0.1	+0.1
6		-0.2	0.0
7			0.0
8			-0.1
9			-0.2
10			-0.3
11			-0.4
12			-0.5

TAXES ON EMPLOYEE ANNUITIES

        The employee annuity is different
from the commercial annuity in only minor
ways. The major differences are:

1. You may have been able to withdraw
    the untaxed portion during the first
    three years of the contract.
2. An alternate simplified procedure
    for calculating the tax on benefits
    is allowed. You may use the method
    that is most favorable to you.
3. If the plan was in effect before
    May 5, 1986 you could draw out your
    taxed contributions before retirement
    and before age 59.5.

4. If your employer has a defined contribution plan and maintains separate accounting for your contributions and the employer contributions, you may draw out your contributions without penalty.
5. If you are a beneficiary to a defined plan of a deceased employee, there is a $5,000 exclusion that may be used to add to the cost of the annuity.

The figures for the number of expected payments of an employee annuity that can be used in the expected return calculations is given below:

AGE AT STARTING DATE	NUMBER OF MONTHLY PAYMENTS
55 and under	300
56 to 60	260
61 to 65	240
66 to 70	170
71 and over	120

COST OF EMPLOYEE ANNUITY

The costs are those of your contributions or those paid by your employer and credited as income to you and on which you paid tax. Other items counted as cost are those pre-1939 contributions of city and state employees, which then were free of income tax. If you had been employed overseas, certain contributions were tax free.

WITHDRAWALS BEFORE STARTING DATE

Withdrawals before a starting date are taxed according to the proportion of untaxed to taxed contributions. Exceptions are points 3 and 4 listed above.

TAXES ON SOCIAL SECURITY PAYMENTS

Your Social Security benefits must be considered in calculating your expected income tax. You will receive a form SSA-1099 by January 31 of each year listing the transactions within your Social Security benefits. These will include Medicare payments, Worker's compensation (if any) and other important items. Mainly there will be a "net benefit" sum that should be used in your tax calculations.

Some general points are:

1.   If you earned more than the allowable, you must reduce your Social Security benefit. In 1992 the reduction is $1.00 of benefit for each $2.00 of earned income over $7,440 if you are under 65. The reduction is $1.00 of benefit for each $3.00 of earned income over $10,200 if you are between 65 and 69 years of age. If you are over 70 years of age there is no reduction. This reduced benefit figure must be used to calculate your taxes. Extra income can signif- cantly increase the taxes. You must pay tax on the earned income that also may increase the tax you pay on Social

Security benefits. In addition the extra income may reduce the Social Security benefits you receive.

2.   Worker's compensation benefits reduce the Social Security benefit. The reduced benefit is used in the tax calculation.

3.   Social Security benefits paid to a child or to an incapacitated dependent are the income of that person.

4.   Non-resident aliens will normally have a 30% tax withheld from 50% of the benefit. Some countries may have tax treaties that do not require the withholding.

5.   The maximum Social Security amount taxed is 50% of the benefit.

6.   If you are still making IRA contribution payments, special calculations must be made since the deductions for IRA payments depend on your income level.

7.   Sometimes a lump sum Social Security benefit payment is made in one calendar year covering amounts due in previous years. You may assume it is a benefit for the current year, or you may recalculate taxes for the previous year for that year's portion and add the tax payment to this year's tax.

8.   The adjusted gross income (increased by non-taxed income and 50% of Social Security benefits) is reduced by a base amount as follows:

```
Single                    $25,000
Married filing jointly     $32,000
Married filing separately $25,000
```

The various effects on taxes are shown by the following examples:

EXAMPLE 1

You are married and have an adjusted gross income from dividends and interest of $25,000 per year. You have $12,000 per year Social Security benefits and $3,000 per year in tax free interest.

```
Adjusted gross income    $25,000
Tax exempt interest        3,000
50% of benefits            6,000
Total                    $34,000

Less base amount          32,000
Excess                     2,000
```

Fifty percent, or $1,000 of this excess of $2,000 is subject to income tax.

EXAMPLE 2.

This example is the same as Example 1, except you are single.

```
Adjusted gross income    $25,000
Tax exempt interest        3,000
50% of benefits            6,000
Total                     34,000
Less base amount          25,000
Excess                     9,000
```

This excess of $9,000 is greater than 50% of the Social Security benefit. Therefore the taxed amount is 50% of $9,000 or $4,500.

HOME SALE TAX EXCLUSION

The tax laws allow profit to be deferred on the sale of a home, provided a new one of equal or greater value is purchased within two years of the sale. Simply moving to a less expensive home can give you a tax liability.

However, if you are over 55 years of age, the government has made an exception. This benefit is an exclusion of $125,000 of profit on the sale of your home. You must have lived in the home for three of the last 5 years. This election is allowed only once in your life time.

This can be a major benefit to you if you meet the requirements and if you have a major price appreciation in the home over your years of ownership. Some people, on retirement, decide to move to a new area or simply buy a new smaller home. Thus, retirement may be the perfect opportunity to sell your old home without the large tax penalty.

Requirements for qualifying for this exclusion are:

1. The owner of the house must be 55 years old by the date of sale. The home ownership must have changed hands after the owner's birthday.

2. If the home is owned jointly by a married couple, it is sufficient for only one spouse to be 55 years of age.

3. The owners must have lived in the house three of the last five years of ownership. A spouse under 55 cannot meet the test by transferring ownership to the joint ownership where the other spouse is over 55.

4. Joint ownership with someone other than a spouse can qualify only if both owners meet the requirements.

5. If the owner is disabled and must be in a licensed care facility, this time can be counted as residence in the house. Short periods of vacation are counted as residence even if the house is rented.

6. Changing you tax election after the sale of your home can generally be made within three years of the due date of income tax filing.

CHAPTER 11

FINANCIAL
TOPICS

A. EARLY RETIREMENT
INCENTIVE OFFERS

Early retirement incentive programs
have become common in the last 10 to 15
years. They are a means for industrial
corporations to reduce their work forces
without the bad publicity and harmful
employee and public relations of normal
layoffs.

If you are offered an early
retirement incentive, you must evaluate
the offer for comparison with your other
alternatives. Alternatives include
continuing at your present job, accepting
another job, going full-time to your
part-time business, working part time
with your work skills, or simply deciding
not to work.

For some of you, the decision will
be easy. If you are near retirement age,
have saved well for this day, and have
been thinking about this for some time,
the extra incentive is like a gift, so
you will take it and run.

IT'S YOUR DECISION

For others the decision may not be
clear. You may be some years from normal
retirement age, the financial package
will give you less than you would have at
normal retirement, and you are not yet
prepared for the life of a retiree. You
must be able to get a handle on the
financial aspects of the offer. Once you
know the financial side you can then
concentrate on the psychological side of
the retirement offer.

These early retirement incentives
are normally offered to employees of a
given age or older within a group of
employees. The offer may be within a
division, a plant, or within a certain
group of employees within the company.
It may exclude certain job functions the
company deems essential.

To avoid discrimination, the offer
must not be coercive and cannot exclude
persons older than the lower age limit
except as explained above. Certain jobs
may be eliminated during the offer
period. This may mean if an individual
does not take the offer, he/she soon may
be terminated. In this case you have
little option but to take the offer.
Sufficient time must be given to make
decisions. One week might not be

considered long enough to reach a
conclusion.

RETIREMENT INCENTIVES

The main goal of an early retirement
program is to bridge the financial gap
between your early retirement date and
your normal retirement date. The gap can
usually be bridged, but often at the
expense of longer term benefits.
Remember that life expectancy plays a big
part in how much money is required to
live the rest of your life on what you
have. If you retire 10 years earlier
than expected, you may need an extra 20
to 30% in your retirement kitty.

Early retirement incentive offers
can contain any of several elements:

1. Adjustments to pensions.
2. Medical insurance incentives.
3. Severance pay.
4. Consulting contracts.
5. Offer of part-time work.
6. Services of a financial advisor
    to help with your decision.
7. Other special incentives.

Your other savings may be the
controlling point in early retirement.
Another 5 to 10 years of work can add
significantly to your savings plans.

DISCUSSION OF RETIREMENT INCENTIVES

A few people may be offered
consulting or part-time contracts. These

contracts may be offered instead of severance pay or some other benefit but are not part of most early retirement incentive offers. This will not be mentioned further.

The services of a financial advisor are usually of very short-term benefit. This advisor can help supply information for your decision, but in the end, only you can make the decision.

Severance pay can range from none to three or four weeks pay per year of service. A common figure is one or two weeks a year of service. This can range from a small part of a year's pay to about two years' pay. This will generally be taxed at your normal tax rate. Severance pay will be at best a minor financial bridge. For some people it may be a bridge for the time it takes to find another job.

PENSION

The intent here is not to cover all aspects of your pension. All are different and you must understand it yourself. The AARP booklet on understanding your pension is an excellent place to start (Reference 1). Another AARP booklet on early retirement incentives is very meager with little important information (Reference 2.)

Adjustments to your pension for early retirement are usually to a level not more than you would receive at normal retirement age and service. They often will be significantly less. The offer may add years to both age and service or may simply add years to the age by some given amount but generally not over age 65.

If you have an early retirement incentive offer before you, the pension is the most important thing to consider. You must get clear information on how much you will receive and what strings are attached. For example, as you reach 65 years of age, it may be reduced by some factor of expected Social Security benefits. The company must make these items clear to you. The hard information you need and must have for a decision should be supplied in writing in the offer. Supplemental information or explanations should be available from your pension administrator.

PENSION QUESTIONS

Some points you must have information on include:

1. When will my payments begin?
2. How long will my payment continue?
3. How does Social Security affect the payment?
4. How much will I receive?
5. Are the benefits adjusted for inflation?
6. How does the age of my spouse affect the benefits?
7. What happens after my death?
8. How are my pension payments guaranteed?
9. Can I roll the annuity over to a more secure trustee?

10. Can I withdraw my pension as a lump sum?
11. What is the tax situation of the pension?
12. If you are under 59 1/2 years old, does the tax surcharge apply?
13. If you go back to work, what happens to the pension payments?
14. Are my payments made monthly, quarterly, or annually?

TYPES OF PENSIONS

Pensions are generally funded in one of two ways--benefit defined or contribution defined. Benefit defined means that money has been paid to a fund in sufficient quantities so some formula will tell you how much you can expect to receive. Defined Contribution benefit plans put money in according to a certain percentage of profits, income, or other factors. When this contribution is added to the income from the fund, you will have a sum in your name. Payments will be taken from your sum according to some formula, which may be partly dependent on the current return. The amount of money you receive each year may vary depending on how well the investments have done.

One recent wrinkle in the pension benefit picture is the financial failure of insurance companies that invested pension fund money in supposedly secure investments, but actually in risky real estate loans or junk bonds. Since these are generally contribution defined plans, the pensioners may have greatly reduced

pension benefits. Other potential
problems are the underfunding of the plan
by an employer, occasionally followed by
bankruptcy. There is no sure thing in
the financial world.

The government does have a pension
insurance program run by the Pension
Benefit Guarantee Corporation. However,
not all plans are insured and not all
features of a plan are insured. Defined
contribution plans are insured only for
the amount in the plan at the time of
bankruptcy. You must check.

The best plan is one that pays you a
lump sum. Then it is up to you to keep
your plan intact and to keep the
investment earning the proper amount.
Even this is not as easy as it may seem.

Just remember the early retirement
offer is a proposal to you. You may
discuss the pension offer with the hope
of changing to more secure funding or
with a guarantee of responsibility of
payment by the employer.

MEDICAL INCENTIVES

The medical incentive is an
increasingly important factor in the
retirement question because of increasing
medical costs. Many of the questions you
have on your pension will apply here.

The major point is how much medical
insurance you will have and how much you
will have to pay for these benefits.
Don't forget that some types of plans
have values up to $10,000 per year for

the years before age 65. Others may have
very little value. A total medical
insurance package with a 1992 value of
$10,000 per year will be equivalent to an
annuity worth over $150,000.

Chapter 8 on Medical Costs and Needs
contains information that may help in
determining if the medical plan offered
is of real value to you. In the worst
case, you may lose your medical coverage,
which will force you to buy your
insurance that could seriously erode the
value of the pension you receive.

If the offer calls for the right to
purchase the group insurance policy at
the company's cost for 18 months, they
are offering you nothing since the law
states they must do this for any employee
that leaves their employment.

Chapter 8 contains much more
information on medical benefits and how
you can judge what you have been offered.

B. SHOULD YOU DRAW SOCIAL SECURITY AT AGE 62?

Most retirees ask themselves if they should draw Social Security when they reach 62 years of age, or wait until age 65. When I retired, I heard rumors that said you should start as early as possible. Others said you should wait until you need the money. I could not find any hard calculations.

The answer to the question depends upon several things. The most important is whether you intend to work, since earned income can seriously lower the amount of benefit. In 1992 if you are between 62 and 65, you can earn up to $7,440 without impact on the Social Security benefit. If you are between 65 and 70 you can earn up to $10,200 without impact. These figures are escalated each year. Up to age 65, earnings above the figure will reduce the Social Security benefit by $1.00 for every $2.00 earned. Between 66 and 70 years of age the reduction is $1.00 for every $3.00 earned. Above age 70 there is no reduction for earned income.

There are many options possible for a retiree and spouse. Typical results are given below. All cases give the same result for any level of benefit.

The only things considered are the Social Security reductions for early withdrawal. The qualified earner's benefits are reduced to 80% of the maximum, at age 62, to 86.7% at age 63, and 93.3% at age 64. The spouse's benefit is 50% of the qualified earner's

at age 65 and 37.5% at age 62. The cost
of living increases were taken at 4% per
year.

A major assumption here is that your
loss is only that from lower benefits due
to age. There is also a lowering of
benefits if, during the years you are not
drawing Social Security, you do not pay
the proportion of Social Security tax
that you have been paying. This is
explained later.

		YEARS TO BREAK EVEN	10% RETURN
1.	Single. Draw age 62 versus age 65	12	27
2	Single Draw age 63 versus age 65	12	29
3.	Single Draw age 64 versus age 65	13	30+
4.	Married Same age. Both draw at age 62 or 65	10	16
5.	Married. Qualified earner draws 62 or 65. Spouse 5 years younger draws at 65	11	18
6.	Married. Qualified earner draws 62 or 65. Spouse 5 years younger draws at 62	11	18

Because of the long times to recover
the losses, it is reasonable to start
drawing benefits as early as possible.
The first 10 to 13 years have a negative
interest so that you lose money during
this period and only reach favorable
returns after 15 to 20 years.

A typical calculation sheet is
presented below. The interest rate can
be viewed as a return on an investment of

the money not received in the first three
years.

Your benefits will further decrease
if you do not contribute Social Security
tax during the years when you do not draw
Social Security benefits. The AIME
(Averaged indexed monthly earnings) will
be lower because of the high maximum
taxable income of the last few years.
Calculations were made assuming benefits
start January 1992, but no Social
Security tax was paid in the previous 1,
2, or 3 years.

```
          DECREASE IN MONTHLY BENEFITS
                          100%     50%
                          AIME     AIME
     NO INCOME
     1991                 $10      $11
     1990, 1991            21       22
     1989, 1990, 1991      30       32
```

These reductions further erode the
benefits of waiting to start Social
Security payments.

C. INCOME FROM INVESTMENTS

This book stated that it is not about investments or how to get the best return on your invested dollar. However, it may be of interest to know how traditional investments have done in the past. Appendix B contains several tables giving historic interest rates and returns on investment. These data start in 1951 and go to 1989. Appendix B-2 gives historic interest rates for several types of bonds and preferred stock. Appendix B-1 gives the rate of change of the consumer price index used as a measure of inflation.

Averages over the entire 49 years are given below with the average for the CPI subtracted from the yield average.

	49 year Avg.	CPI 49 year Avg.	DIFF.
Municipal bonds	5.50%	4.33%	1.17
Long tm. cp. bonds	6.89	4.33	2.53
Long tm. gvt. bonds	6.44	4.33	2.11
Pref. stock yields	6.92	4.33	2.59

You may note the highest yield over inflation was 2.59% per year. The results of same calculations are below for the last 15 years of data.

	15 year Avg.	CPI 15 year Avg.	DIFF.
Municipal bonds	8.10%	6.31%	1.79
Long tm. cp. bonds	10.20	6.31	3.89
Long tm. gvt. bonds	9.82	6.31	3.51
Pref.stock yields	9.68	6.31	3.37

Over the last 15 years, the yield over inflation rate ranged to a high of

3.89%. If you invest in these safe securities, do not over estimate what you might get in yield.

The same type of data can be calculated from the figures in Appendix B-3, which give the annual change in price and the annual dividend rate of the Standard and Poor's 500 stock index. The last column gives the sum of the dividend rate and the annual price change in percent that represents the total return on the stocks.

	49 YEAR AVG.	15 YEAR AVG.
TOTAL RETURN (49 YEARS)	10.55%	12.54%
CPI AVERAGE INCREASE	4.33	6.31
DIFFERENCE	6.22%	6.23%

This shows that equity stocks have a significant edge in long term return over bonds. The pitfall of stock ownership is the very wide swings that occur on a short term basis.

D. SPENDING AND INCOME PATTERNS OF THE ABOVE AGE 65 POPULATION

The Bureau of Labor Statistics makes surveys of the population to get income and spending patterns for different age groups. They use the term "Reference person" to represent a household unit, be it one person, two persons or a family. The data in the following tables represent the 1987 survey. These data are from responses from 2,727 consumer units. The data given represent the "median" that signifies one-half the values are above the figure and one half are below the figure. In this way a single high roller cannot skew the data.

AVERAGE ANNUAL INCOME AND EXPENDITURES
DOLLARS   (1987)

	INCOME BEFORE TAXES	TOTAL EXPEND.	FOOD TOTAL
All consumers	$27,326	$24,414	$3,664
Under 25 years	12,621	14,368	2,204
25 - 34 years	27,835	24,177	3,567
35 - 44 years	36,240	31,473	4,638
45 - 54 years	36,941	31,708	4,625
55 - 64 years	31,038	25,707	3,887
65 - 74 years	18,598	18,888	2,971
75 years & up	12,912	12,230	2,104

Since we are interested in the retirement age groups, the expenditures of the 65 to 74 and the 75 + age groups were further analyzed for expenditures.

EXPENDITURE DISTRIBUTION

Age group	65 - 74	75 +
Total Income	$18,598	$12,912
Total Expenditures	18,888	12,230
Total Food	2,971	2,104
At home	1,897	1,496
Away from home	1,074	609
Alcohol	164	74
Housing	5,965	4,521
Apparel and Service	1,035	545
Transportation		
Purchases	1,269	422
Gasoline/oil	667	332
Other trans.	1,338	639
Health Care	1,688	1,596
Pensions/Soc.Sec.	610	139
Other	3,179	1,856
Personal Taxes	961	632

"Other" includes miscellaneous items such as insurance, entertainment, personal care, reading, education, smoking supplies and contributions.

This same 1987 data was analyzed by Walker and Schwenk (Reference 20) to give the income ranges of the age groups.

INCOME DISTRIBUTION
PERCENT

	70-79	80 +	All ages
Under $5,000	12.3	16.5	9.2
$5,000 - $9,999	35.2	43.9	15.4
$10,000 - $14,999	20.3	17.1	12.8
$15,000 - $19,999	11.4	7.8	10.3
$20,000 - $29,999	10.2	7.4	17.5
$30,000 - $39,999	4.9	3.0	13.0
$40,000 and over	5.7	4.3	21.8

The sources of income for the two different age groups were as follows:

| | MEAN | |
SOURCE	AGE 70 -79	AGE 80 +
WAGES AND SALARIES	$1,908	$1,171
NET BUSINESS	490	146
NET FARM	51	-
SOCIAL SECURITY, RAILROAD RETIREMENT, AND PRIVATE RETIREMENT		
SOC. SEC. & R.R. RET.	7,711	6,899
PENSIONS AND ANNUITIES	2,406	1,524
INTEREST, DIVIDEND, PROPERTY INCOME.		
DIVIDENDS, TRUSTS, ROY.	678	725
INTEREST ON SAVING, BONDS	1,482	1,809
ROOMER AND BOARDER INCOME	6	
OTHER RENTAL INCOME	126	65
PUBLIC ASSISTANCE		
WELFARE	14	-
SUPPLEMENTAL SECURITY INC.	107	65
FOOD STAMPS	32	18
OTHER INCOME		
REGULAR CONTRIBUTIONS	33	34
OTHER MONEY INCOME	61	-
TOTAL INCOME (BEFORE TAXES)	15,174	12,627
TOTAL INCOME (AFTER TAXES)	14,402	12,083

The expenditures of the same two age groups from the same study are:

MEDIAN EXPENDITURES

	AGE 70 - 79 $	%	AGE 80 + $	%
FOOD	2,618	18	1,890	19
HOUSING	4,864	34	4,162	42
TRANSPORTATION	2,577	18	1,010	10
HEATH CARE	1,626	11	1,432	14
APPAREL AND SERV.	615	4	288	3
ENTERTAINMENT	519	4	231	2
PERSONAL CARE	190	1	159	2
READING	133	1	84	1
EDUCATION	18	0	10	0
MISCELLANEOUS	291	2	165	2
CASH CONTRIBUTIONS	169	1	222	2
INSURANCE AND RET.	518	4	249	2
ALCOHOL	123	1	43	0
TOBACCO	134	1	68	1
TOTAL EXPEND.	$14,397		$10,015	

An interesting point from these data is the above 80 year old person was still saving over $2,000 per year.

ASSETS OF PERSONS

ABOVE 65 YEARS OF AGE

Another approach to the financial well being of the over 65 age group is to consider the assets they have. The Census Bureau makes a survey of assets of persons over age 65, through their Survey of Income and Program Participation (SIPP). Reference 10 was used here as the source of these data.

```
                    NET WORTH
    AGE GROUP                       MEDIAN
    35 AND UNDER                    $ 6,000
    35 - 44                          33,200
    45 - 54                          57,500
    55 - 64                          80,000
    65 - 69                          83,500
    70 - 74                          82,100
    75 AND OLDER                     61,500
```

The data were further broken down by quintiles for the above 65 age category.

```
    LOWEST 20%    LESS THAN    $15,041
    NEXT 20%      $15,042 TO   $49,420
    MID 20%       $49,420 TO   $84,625
    NEXT 20%      $84,625 TO   $147,450
    HIGHEST 20%   ABOVE        $147,450
```

Incomes of the above 65 group are lower than, for example, the 45 to 54 age, but they control significantly more of the assets.

Several points brought out by the authors are:

1. When the 1988 results were compared with the 1984 results, the above 65 age groups increased in assets while the assets of the below 65 age groups decreased.

2. There is a large difference between the highest and lowest groups.

3. The main difference between the poorest and next poorest, is ownership or at least an interest in a house and car.

4. There was a very strong correlation between education and net worth.

5. People now entering the retired category are from the era when there was a very large increase in educational attainment, so that there is a good probability they will have higher assets.

E. POPULATION TRENDS IN THE UNITED STATES

The United States has been experiencing a growth in the older end of the population for many years. The growth of the total population and in the above 65 and above 80 age groups with the projections to the year 2025 are given below. The data is from U.S. Bureau of Census as reported by the Bureau of Labor Statistics.

POPULATION IN THOUSANDS

YEAR	TOTAL POPULATION	ABOVE AGE 65	ABOVE AGE 85
1960	179,323	16,675	2,541
1970	203,302	20,107	3,742
1980	226,546	25,704	5,223
1990	250,410	31,559	7,108
2000	268,266	34,882	9,357
2025	298,252	59,713	13,658

The above table shows that one person in eight is over 65 years of age. The projections for the year 2025 are that one person in five will be age 65 or older. This trend toward more and more people of retirement age will surely bring major changes in political and social areas in the future and probably in our life time.

The distribution of above age 65 population is further expanded in the following table: (1990 and 2000 are projections based on 1988 and previous years' figures).

PERCENTAGES BY AGE GROUP

	1960	1970	1980	1990	2000
65 & over	100.0	100.0	100.0	100.0	100.0
65 - 69	37.7	34.9	34.3	32.5	27.2
70 - 74	28.6	27.2	26.6	25.7	25.1
75 - 79	18.5	19.3	18.8	19.3	20.9
80 - 84	9.6	11.5	11.5	12.1	13.6
85 & over	5.6	7.1	8.8	10.3	13.3

Of significant interest to those of us in the early part of this table is the big increase in the over 85 age category. This is telling us we have an increasing chance of living past age 85. In 1990, 1 in 10 of the people age 65 and over is older than 85 years of age. In the year 2000, 1 in 7.5 will be over age 85. By the year 2025, of the over age 65 population, 1 in 4.4 will be over 80 years of age. The Bureau of Census projects in this same year, 4.6% of the total population will be over 80 years of age. (My comments are they may be low because of the tremendous advances now being made in medicine.)

The good news for women, and bad for men, is much of the increase in numbers of persons that live longer will be with the female population. The table below shows the ratio of females to males for each age group.

RATIO OF WOMEN TO MEN

	1960	1970	1980	1990	2000
65 & over	1.21	1.39	1.48	1.46	1.44
65 - 69	1.14	1.24	1.25	1.20	1.17
70 - 74	1.17	1.35	1.32	1.31	1.27
75 - 79	1.25	1.46	1.54	1.53	1.45
80 - 84	1.38	1.62	1.88	1.84	1.72
85 & over	1.57	1.88	2.30	2.54	2.49

The projections for the years 1990 and 2000 show a reversal in trend of the ratio of women to men. The bureaucratic powers must see something not apparent from these data.

F. COMPARISON OF TAXED AND TAX DEFERRED SAVINGS

The Federal government has recognized the need for saving incentives to aid people in retirement. To this end they have created many tax deferred plans. These plans can be lumped into two categories with a third being the normal savings.

1. Both payments and principal are tax deferred.
2. Payments to the plan are taxed but the interest is tax deferred.
3. Both payments and interest are taxed.

To show the tax impact, a series of calculations can be made for each case. The following table shows the results for $1,000 per year before taxes put into each account. The appropriate taxes are then paid from each account as they accrue.

YEARS	ALL TAX DEFERRED	TAX DEFERRED ON INTEREST	ALL TAXED
10	$15,645	$12,203	$11,046
(A.T.)	12,203	11,233	11,046
20	49,423	38,549	31,281
(A.T.)	38,550	33,500	31,281
30	122,346	95,430	68,348
(A.T.)	95,430	79,583	68,348

"A.T." signifies the amount of money left after withdrawing and paying taxes. The tax rate was taken at 22% reflecting a 15% Federal tax and a 7% State tax. An

8% interest rate was assumed. Withdrawal
was taken without age penalty.

PERCENT BENEFIT
TOTALLY TAX DEFERRED SAVINGS

YEARS	OVER ONLY INTEREST DEFERRED	OVER TOTALLY TAXED
10	8.6%	10.5%
20	15.0	23.2
30	19.9	39.6

G. ADVANTAGE OF TIME IN SAVINGS

The advantage of time to accumulate savings cannot be overestimated. Compounding of interest is a tremendous benefit. This can best be illustrated by example. You have the choice of putting $1,000 per year into a savings plan for 20 years or you can delay 10 years and put in $2,000 per year into a plan for 10 years. In each case you put $20,000 into the account. Assume an 8% interest on the money and that no taxes are paid. A table showing the two cases is on the next page.

In the first column the $20,000 has more than doubled while the second column shows the $20,000 has only increased by 50%. This is a tremendous financial advantage.

The argument against it is that the early dollars were worth more since inflation erodes purchasing power. However the interest rate more than compensates for inflation.

YEAR	$1,000 YEAR 1 VALUE	$2,000 YEAR 11 VALUE
1	$1,080.00	$0.00
2	$2,166.40	$0.00
3	$3,339.71	$0.00
4	$4,606.89	$0.00
5	$5,975.44	$0.00
6	$7,453.48	$0.00
7	$9,049.75	$0.00
8	$10,773.73	$0.00
9	$12,635.63	$0.00
10	$14,646.48	$0.00
11	$16,818.20	$2,160.00
12	$19,163.66	$4,332.80
13	$21,696.75	$6,679.42
14	$24,432.49	$9,213.78
15	$27,387.09	$11,950.88
16	$30,578.06	$14,906.95
17	$34,024.30	$18,099.51
18	$37,746.25	$21,547.47
19	$41,765.94	$25,271.26
20	$46,107.22	$29,292.97

H.   FIRST WITHDRAWALS FROM ALREADY TAXED FUNDS

To illustrate the effect of drawing money from already taxed accounts first, consider the following examples.

Start with $100,000 in a tax deferred account and $100,000 in a taxed account. Assume both earn interest at 8% a year. From the total of $200,000 draw out enough to have $15,000 per year after paying all taxes. Assume a marginal tax rate of 15% and an interest rate of 8%. Assume funds are withdrawn at end of year to make the calculations easier. All relevant taxes are also paid at the end of the year.

CASE 1.   Withdraw funds from tax deferred account first and then switch to the already taxed account when funds from the tax deferred account are depleted.

The tax deferred account will be depleted in the eighth year. The value of the taxed account will have grown to $164,000. After 25 years there will remain $67,000 in the taxed account.

CASE 2.   Withdraw funds from the taxed account first letting the tax deferred account grow until the taxed fund is exhausted when you start drawing from the tax deferred account.

The taxed account will be depleted in the tenth year and withdrawal will begin from the

tax deferred account. The tax
deferred account will have grown
to $200,000. After 25 years
there is still $164,000 in the
tax deferred account.

In the particular case illustrated
here there is an after-tax gain to you of
$61,150.14 over the 25-year period by
drawing taxed funds first. This is a gain
of 13.8% in money over the period. This
is 30.6% based on the original $200,000.
You should make every effort to apply
this principle.

The benefits are primarily from the
interest on the delay in paying taxes,
not in the lower taxes themselves. The
highest total at the end of the period
paid the most in taxes. However, the
taxes were paid later in the 25-year
period.

TABLE 1

WITHDRAW TAX DEFERRED MONEY FIRST
CASE 1

YEAR	PRINCIPAL	INTEREST	TAXES	WITHDRAWN
1	200,000.00	16,000.00	3,847.00	18,847.00
2	197,153.00	15,772.24	3,928.60	18,928.60
3	193,996.64	15,519.73	4,015.75	19,015.75
4	190,500.62	15,240.05	4,108.82	19,108.82
5	186,631.85	14,930.55	4,208.23	19,208.23
6	182,354.17	14,588.33	4,314.39	19,314.39
7	177,628.11	14,210.25	4,427.77	19,427.77
8	172,410.59	13,792.85	4,156.67	19,156.67
9	167,046.76	13,363.74	2,004.56	17,004.56
10	163,405.94	13,072.48	1,960.87	16,960.87
11	159,517.54	12,761.40	1,914.21	16,914.21
12	155,364.74	12,429.18	1,864.38	16,864.38
13	150,929.54	12,074.36	1,811.15	16,811.15
14	146,192.75	11,695.42	1,754.31	16,754.31
15	141,133.85	11,290.71	1,693.61	16,693.61
16	135,730.96	10,858.48	1,628.77	16,628.77
17	129,960.66	10,396.85	1,559.53	16,559.53
18	123,797.99	9,903.84	1,485.58	16,485.58
19	117,216.25	9,377.30	1,406.59	16,406.59
20	110,186.95	8,814.96	1,322.24	16,322.24
21	102,679.67	8,214.37	1,232.16	16,232.16
22	94,661.88	7,572.95	1,135.94	16,135.94
23	86,098.89	6,887.91	1,033.19	16,033.19
24	76,953.62	6,156.29	923.44	15,923.44
25	67,186.46	5,374.92	806.24	15,806.24
WITHDRAWAL			0	67,186.46

TOTAL TAXES PAID $58,544.00

The sum of $67,186.46 can be withdrawn and used without paying further taxes. The total money withdrawn was $15,000 per year for 25 years ($375,000) plus the final sum of $67,186.46 for a total of $442,186.46.

TABLE 2

WITHDRAW ALREADY TAXED MONEY FIRST
CASE 2

YEAR	PRINCIPAL	INTEREST	TAX	WITHDRAWAL
1	200,000.00	16,000.00	1,200.00	16,200.00
2	199,800.00	15,984.00	1,101.60	16,101.60
3	199,682.40	15,974.59	996.51	15,996.51
4	199,660.48	15,972.84	884.27	15,884.27
5	199,749.05	15,979.92	764.40	15,764.40
6	199,964.57	15,997.17	636.38	15,636.38
7	200,325.36	16,026.03	499.66	15,499.66
8	200,851.73	16,068.14	353.63	15,353.63
9	201,566.24	16,125.30	197.68	15,197.68
10	202,493.86	16,199.51	2,189.67	17,189.86
11	201,503.51	16,120.28	2,647.00	17,647.00
12	199,976.78	15,998.14	2,647.00	17,647.00
13	198,327.92	15,866.23	2,647.00	17,647.00
14	196,547.16	15,723.77	2,647.00	17,647.00
15	194,623.93	15,569.91	2,647.00	17,647.00
16	192,546.84	15,403.75	2,647.00	17,647.00
17	190,303.59	15,224.29	2,647.00	17,647.00
18	187,880.88	15,030.47	2,647.00	17,647.00
19	185,264.35	14,821.15	2,647.00	17,647.00
20	182,438.50	14,595.08	2,647.00	17,647.00
21	179,386.57	14,350.93	2,647.00	17,647.00
22	176,090.50	14,087.24	2,647.00	17,647.00
23	172,530.74	13,802.46	2,647.00	17,647.00
24	168,686.20	13,494.90	2,647.00	17,647.00
25	164,534.10	13,162.73	2,647.00	17,647.00
WITHDRAWAL			36,197.50	128,336.60
	TOTAL TAXES PAID		84,726.30	

The sum of $164,534.10 can be withdrawn and used if taxes are paid. At a 22% tax rate this would leave a net of $128,336.60. The total after tax money withdrawn was $15,000 each year for 25 years ($375,000) plus the final lump sum for a total of $503,336.60.

I. REVERSE MORTGAGES

Some people may have a sizeable asset in their home, but not have sufficient money to live on. A reverse mortgage, in theory, gives this person the ability to have their cake and eat it too. In other words, keep the home until you die or move, but get money for what the house is worth. The reverse mortgage is officially known as a HOME EQUITY CONVERSION MORTGAGE (HECM).

A reverse mortgage is a contract with a bank or other lending institution where you sell them your home, but with the stipulation you live in it until you die, move, or for a fixed period of time. In return the lending organization will pay you monthly payments or provide for a line of credit.

There is little experience with this type of mortgage, so some points may not be totally clear. For example in summer of 1991 only three North Carolina firms offered these loans.

To be eligible for a reverse mortgage the home must be paid for or with very little remaining to be paid. In addition the home-owner must be 62 or older with very little else in the way of assets.

Based on the age of the home-owner and the value of the house, different plan options may be available. Some stipulations are common to these loans.

1. Repayment of the loan is not required during the home-owner's occupation of the home.

2. A home-owner cannot be forced to sell the home even if the payments exceed the home value.

3. The loan balance including interest becomes due and payable when the home-owner moves or dies.

4. The heirs are liable for the loan only up to the fair market value of the home.

5. If the home has a value greater than the loan principal the heirs (or home-owner) may sell the home to pay off the note and keep the balance.

In 1991 the Federal National Mortgage Association allocated $2 billion to this type of loan, so if you meet the requirements you may want to investigate this option.

A pitfall of the reverse mortgage is when the owner leaves the home the loan becomes due and no further payments are made. One company is claiming to be making plans to offer reverse mortgages where payments are made for the life of the insured even if they live to be 100 years old.

J. COST OF OWNING NON-PRODUCTIVE ASSETS

There are many luxury items where the asset has a value but produces no or little income. Most of these types of items cost money to maintain, use, or operate. Examples are such items as second homes that are not rented, a yacht for personal use, or expensive pieces of jewelry.

Several examples are given below showing how much your six weekends a year in your mountain home in the Smokies cost you. You can then make your decision on whether to sell and convert to a cash earning asset or to keep for your enjoyment.

EXAMPLE 1

Assume you own a vacation home in the Smokies with a market value of $70,000. The mortgage is paid off.

The annual operating costs are as follows:

Utilities	$1,000/yr.
Maintenance	500
Insurance	400
Property Taxes	600
TOTAL	$2,500/yr.

Taxes are deductible. You are in the 22% tax bracket (15% Federal plus 7% state) so that you "Save" $600 x 0.22 = $132/yr.

The net out-of-pocket expense is therefore $2,500 - $132 or $2,368/yr.

However, the $70,000 has a net loss
of interest (assuming an interest rate of
8%/yr) of $5,600/yr. If you assume you
take the principal to zero over your life
expectancy of 25 years, the principal
cost is $6,558/yr. These figures are
before paying taxes, which depends on the
taxed and non-taxed portion of the
equity. If we assume no price
appreciation, this figure is not taxed.

Thus, your costs of owning this
second home are:

```
Principal intact    $2,368 + 5,660 =
                             $8,028/yr.
Deplete principal   $2,368 + 6,558 =
                             $8,926/yr.
```

EXAMPLE 2

Consider the same house, except that
it is being paid off with a 15-year note
at 7.5% interest. This note has just
been through its tenth year so that five
years of payments remain. The house will
be totally paid for in December of 1996.
The payments on the $40,000 note are
$370.81/mo. or $4,444.92/yr.

```
Principal Jan. 1, 1992      $18,504.24
Payments in 1992              4,444.92
Interest paid 1992            1,280.34
Paid to Principal 1992        3,169.38
Principal Jan. 1, 1993       15,334.86
```

Both taxes and interest are
deductible at the same 22% tax rate for a
tax savings of $281.67 on the interest
and $132 savings on the taxes for a total
tax savings of $413.67 in 1992.

The out-of-pocket cost in 1992 is:

Mortgage	$4,444.92
Operating cost	2,500.00
Tax benefit	− 413.67
TOTAL	$6,531.25

Equity in home Jan. 1, 1993

$70,000 − 15334.86 = $54,665.14

However, the $54,665.14 also has a net loss of income (assuming an interest rate of 8%/yr) of $4,373.21/yr. If you assume you take the principle to zero over your life expectancy taken at 25 years, the principle cost is $6,558/yr. These figures are before paying taxes that are assumed to be zero, since the money has already been taxed.

Thus, your cost of owning this second home is:

Principal intact
   $6,531 + 4,373 = $10,904/yr.
Deplete principal
   $6,531 + 6,558 = $13,089/yr.

These figures should be reduced by $3,169, which is the amount going to equity in this year. These figures will be slowly reduced as you make your home payments until they become the same as in EXAMPLE 1.

Several points to be made here are:

1.   You can develop the figures for your particular situation and event.
2.   You can include gains and losses.
3.   You must determine if your use of the facility is worth the cost.

4. The main idea here is to recognize
    the situation so that you can make a
    decision.
5. Most people keep these type items
    and sell only as a last resort.

EXAMPLE 3

You sometimes want to know exactly
what the house of Example 1 cost you to
acquire.

Assume you purchased the house in
January 1, 1976 for $55,000 with a down
payment of $15,000 and a $40,000
mortgage. The mortgage was a 15-year
note at 7.5% interest resulting in
monthly payments of $370.81 per month of
$4,444.92 per year. Closing costs,
lawyer fees, surveying costs, and other
fees added another $1000 to the initial
cost.

The note was paid off effective
January 1, 1991.

Total initial cost $16,000

From Appendix A-2 the compound sum
of $1.00 at 8% interest over 15 years is
3.172. This figure is 1.08 to the 15th
power that is easily calculated on a hand
calculator. Thus, if the $16,000 were
invested over this 15 years at 8%
interest it would have a present value of
$50,752 (3.172 x 16,000).

Assume the mortgage payments and the
operating costs were invested in an
account that paid 8% on money in the
account. Also assume that the sum was
put into the account at the beginning of
each year.

The net amount should be adjusted for the tax savings, which will vary each year. Tax laws have changed that were more favorable to owning a house but for purposes here assume the 7th year to calculate tax on the interest paid. The interest of $2100 gives a tax savings of $462 per year. Added to the $132 tax savings on property taxes gives $594 per year in total tax benefit. Thus, the total spent each year (average) is $4444.92 + 2,500.00 - 594.00 = $6,350.92 per year.

For this case Appendix A-3 gives the values called "Sum of an Annuity of $1 for N periods. Taking the value for 8% and 15 years you will find a figure of 27.152. Thus, the $6350.92 per year will amount to $172,440 ($6,350.92 x 27.152).

Total cost:

Initial payment	$50,752
Mortgage/oper. payments	177,572
Increase in property value	
Current value $70,000	
Initial value 55,000	
	-15,000
Net cost of this property	$213,324

If this home is kept another 10 years the cost of this $70,000 invested at 8% per year is an additional $151,130. The property value may increase some but not this much. Don't wait too long to act.

CONCLUSION

This book has shown you how to retire and make your money last for the rest of your life. If you have been working through each step in this book, you should now have a clear financial picture for your and your spouse's financial security during your retirement years. You have:

- Developed a list of assets, considering all income generating items and non-liquid assets

- Calculated your income from these assets, accounting for inflation, interest rates, and your and your spouse's life expectancy

- Estimated your annual expenses

- Found the gap between your income and expenses

- Found ways to reduce living costs to eliminate any negative gap

From time to time, your income and expenses may change. Inflation and interest rates will fluctuate. It will, therefore, be necessary to return to these steps and update your figures periodically. However, you have

developed a system for understanding and
budgeting your retirement income.

So, enjoy retirement. Sleep late.
Be your own boss. Visit the
grandchildren. Travel to the places
you've always wanted to visit. Do what
you want to do when you want to do it.
And enjoy the peace of mind that comes
from financial security.

REFERENCES

1. American Association of Retired People. (1989). <u>A Guide to Understanding Your Pension Plan.</u> Washinton, DC: Author.

2. American Association of Retired People. (1988). <u>Look Before You Leap.</u> Washington, DC: Author.

3. Blankson,I. & Powell, K. (1991). <u>How To Plan and Invest For Your Retirement.</u> Stamford, CT: Longmeadow Press.

4. Detlefs, D. R., & Myers, R. J. (1991). <u>Your Guide To Social Security Benefits.</u> Louisville, KY: Mercer.

5. Gladney, G. (1991). <u>Understanding Insurance.</u> Stamford CT: Longmeadow Press.

6. Gordon, H., & David, J. (1991). <u>How to Protect Your Life Savings From Catastrophic Illness and Nursiing Homes.</u> Boston: Financial Planning Institute.

7. J.K.Lasser Tax Institute Staff. (1991). <u>J.K. Lasser's Your Income Tax 1992.</u> New York: Prentice Hall.

8. J.K.Lasser Institute Staff. (1988). J.K. Lasser's 1989-1990 Retirement Plan Handbook. New York: J.K. Lasser Institute.

9. Koenig, R. H. (1991). How To Lower Your Property Taxes. New York: Fireside.

10. Longino, C.F.,& Crown, W. H. (1991, August). Older Americans: Rich Or Poor? American Demographics, p 48.

11. McLean, A. J. (1991). How To Retire On The House. Chicago: Contemporary Books.

12. Petras, K., & Petras, R. (1991). The Only Retirement Guide You'll Ever Need. New York: Poseidon Press.

13. Pond, J. D. (1991). Personalised Financial Planning Guide For Self-Employed Professionals and Small Business Owners,. New York: Dell.

14. Porter, S. (1976). Money Book. New York: Avon.

15. Rubin, L. G. (1991). Your 1991/1992 Guide To Social Security Benefits., New York: Facts On File.

16. Simmons, L., & Simmons, B. (1991). Penny Pinching. New York: Bantam Non-Fiction.

17. Statistical Service, (1990). Security Price Index Record., New York: Standard and Poor's: Author.

18. U. S. Bureau of Labor Statistics, (1991, August). _CPI Detailed Report._ Washington, DC: U. S. Government Printing Office.

19. U. S. Bureau of Labor Statistics, (1991). _Statistics Of The United States._ Washington, DC: U. S. Government Printing Office.

20. Walker, R. S., & Schwenk, F. N. (1991). Income and Expenditure Patterns Of Consumer Units With Reference Persons Age 70 To 79 And 85 And Older. _Family Economic Review._ 4, (1), 8 -13.

21. Weston, J. F., & Bingham, E. F. (1974). _Essentials Of Managerial Finance._ Hinsdale, IL: The Dryden Press.

APPENDIX A

FINANCIAL TABLES

APPENDIX A-1   200

    DESCRIPTION OF
    FINANCIAL TABLES

APPENDIX A-2   203

    COMPOUND VALUE OF $1.00

APPENDIX A-3   204

    SUM OF AN ANNUITY

APPENDIX A-4   205

    PRESENT VALUE OF $1.00

APPENDIX A-5   206

    PRESENT VALUE
    OF AN ANNUITY

APPENDIX A-1

DESCRIPTION OF FINANCIAL TABLES

APPENDIX A-2

COMPOUND VALUE OF $1.00

$1.00 invested at time zero, at R% interest compounded annually, for N years. Compounded annually means the interest is added to the principal at the end of each year.

The mathematical relationship between the various factors is given below:

    A = amount after N years
    R = interest rate as decimal
    P = initial payment
    N = Time, years

$$A = P \times (1 + R)^N$$

APPENDIX A-3

SUM OF AN ANNUITY

This table gives the value of $1.00 invested each year for N years in a plan at R% interest compounded annually. Payment is made at the end of each year.

The mathematical relationship of the various factors is as follows:

```
A = amount after N years
R = interest rate as decimal
P = Annual payment
N = Time, years

A = P x [(1 + R)^N - 1]/R
```

APPENDIX A-4

PRESENT VALUE OF $1.00

This table gives the present value of $1.00 due in N years at R% interest. In different words, it is the amount that you must invest today to have $1.00 in N years with R% interest compounded annually.

```
A = amount after N years
R = interest rate as decimal
P = present value
N = Time, years

P = A/(1 + R)^N
```

APPENDIX A-5

PRESENT VALUE OF AN ANNUITY

The tables of this appendix represent the amount of money that must be set aside today, at a compounded interest rate, to make annual payments for N years. Payments are made at the end of the year.

Table 1 is for a fixed payment of $1,000, for N years at R% interest compounded annually.

Tables 2 through 8 represent the
same information except that the $1,000
is escalated annually by the escalation
rate indicated.

APPENDIX A-2

COMPOUND VALUE OF $1

PERIOD	4%	5%	6%	7%	8%	9%	10%
1	1.0400	1.0500	1.0600	1.0700	1.0800	1.0900	1.1000
2	1.0816	1.1025	1.1236	1.1449	1.1664	1.1881	1.2100
3	1.1249	1.1576	1.1910	1.2250	1.2597	1.2950	1.3310
4	1.1699	1.2155	1.2625	1.3108	1.3605	1.4116	1.4641
5	1.2167	1.2763	1.3382	1.4026	1.4693	1.5386	1.6105
6	1.2653	1.3401	1.4185	1.5007	1.5869	1.6771	1.7716
7	1.3159	1.4071	1.5036	1.6058	1.7138	1.8280	1.9487
8	1.3686	1.4775	1.5938	1.7182	1.8509	1.9926	2.1436
9	1.4233	1.5513	1.6895	1.8385	1.9990	2.1719	2.3579
10	1.4802	1.6289	1.7908	1.9672	2.1589	2.3674	2.5937
11	1.5395	1.7103	1.8983	2.1049	2.3316	2.5804	2.8531
12	1.6010	1.7959	2.0122	2.2522	2.5182	2.8127	3.1384
13	1.6651	1.8856	2.1329	2.4098	2.7196	3.0658	3.4523
14	1.7317	1.9799	2.2609	2.5785	2.9372	3.3417	3.7975
15	1.8009	2.0789	2.3966	2.7590	3.1722	3.6425	4.1772
16	1.8730	2.1829	2.5404	2.9522	3.4259	3.9703	4.5950
17	1.9479	2.2920	2.6928	3.1588	3.7000	4.3276	5.0545
18	2.0258	2.4066	2.8543	3.3799	3.9960	4.7171	5.5599
19	2.1068	2.5270	3.0256	3.6165	4.3157	5.1417	6.1159
20	2.1911	2.6533	3.2071	3.8697	4.6610	5.6044	6.7275
25	2.6658	3.3864	4.2919	5.4274	6.8485	8.6231	10.8347
30	3.2434	4.3219	5.7435	7.6123	10.0627	13.2677	17.4494

APPENDIX A-3

SUM OF AN ANNUITY

$1 FOR N PERIODS

$1 DEPOSITED AT INTEREST SHOWN
FOR N PERIODS
PAYMENT AT END OF PERIOD

PERIOD	4%	6%	8%	10%	12%	14%
1	1.0000	1.0000	1.0000	1.0000	1.0000	1.0000
2	2.0400	2.0600	2.0800	2.1000	2.1200	2.1400
3	3.1216	3.1836	3.2464	3.3100	3.3744	3.4396
4	4.2465	4.3746	4.5061	4.6410	4.7793	4.9211
5	5.4163	5.6371	5.8666	6.1051	6.3528	6.6101
6	6.6330	6.9753	7.3359	7.7156	8.1152	8.5355
7	7.8983	8.3938	8.9228	9.4872	10.0890	10.7305
8	9.2142	9.8975	10.6366	11.4359	12.2997	13.2328
9	10.5828	11.4913	12.4876	13.5795	14.7757	16.0853
10	12.0061	13.1808	14.4866	15.9374	17.5487	19.3373
11	13.4864	14.9716	16.6455	18.5312	20.6546	23.0445
12	15.0258	16.8699	18.9771	21.3843	24.1331	27.2707
13	16.6268	18.8821	21.4953	24.5227	28.0291	32.0887
14	18.2919	21.0151	24.2149	27.9750	32.3926	37.5811
15	20.0236	23.2760	27.1521	31.7725	37.2797	43.8424
16	21.8245	25.6725	30.3243	35.9497	42.7533	50.9804
17	23.6975	28.2129	33.7502	40.5447	48.8837	59.1176
18	25.6454	30.9057	37.4502	45.5992	55.7497	68.3941
19	27.6712	33.7600	41.4463	51.1591	63.4397	78.9692
20	29.7781	36.7856	45.7620	57.2750	72.0524	91.0249
25	41.6459	54.8645	73.1059	98.3471	133.3339	181.8708
30	56.0849	79.0582	113.2832	164.4940	241.3327	356.7868

APPENDIX A-4

PRESENT VALUE OF $1

PERIOD	3%	4%	5%	6%	7%	8%
1	0.9709	0.9615	0.9524	0.9434	0.9346	0.9259
2	0.9426	0.9246	0.9070	0.8900	0.8734	0.8573
3	0.9151	0.8890	0.8638	0.8396	0.8163	0.7938
4	0.8885	0.8548	0.8227	0.7921	0.7629	0.7350
5	0.8626	0.8219	0.7835	0.7473	0.7130	0.6806
6	0.8375	0.7903	0.7462	0.7050	0.6663	0.6302
7	0.8131	0.7599	0.7107	0.6651	0.6227	0.5835
8	0.7894	0.7307	0.6768	0.6274	0.5820	0.5403
9	0.7664	0.7026	0.6446	0.5919	0.5439	0.5002
10	0.7441	0.6756	0.6139	0.5584	0.5083	0.4632
11	0.7224	0.6496	0.5847	0.5268	0.4751	0.4289
12	0.7014	0.6246	0.5568	0.4970	0.4440	0.3971
13	0.6810	0.6006	0.5303	0.4688	0.4150	0.3677
14	0.6611	0.5775	0.5051	0.4423	0.3878	0.3405
15	0.6419	0.5553	0.4810	0.4173	0.3624	0.3152
16	0.6232	0.5339	0.4581	0.3936	0.3387	0.2919
17	0.6050	0.5134	0.4363	0.3714	0.3166	0.2703
18	0.5874	0.4936	0.4155	0.3503	0.2959	0.2502
19	0.5703	0.4746	0.3957	0.3305	0.2765	0.2317
20	0.5537	0.4564	0.3769	0.3118	0.2584	0.2145
25	0.4776	0.3751	0.2953	0.2330	0.1842	0.1460
30	0.4120	0.3083	0.2314	0.1741	0.1314	0.0994

APPENDIX A-5

PRESENT VALUE OF AN ANNUITY

An annuity is a sum of money set aside to pay periodic payments for a given number of years.

Tables are given below showing the amount that must be set aside to draw an annual payment for the number of years shown and at the interest rate given.

The first table is with a fixed $1,000 a year payment. The others are for a $1,000 a year payment the first year but escalated by a given percentage each year thereafter. This percentage is labeled "escalation rate" in the tables.

TABLE 1

ESCALATION RATE   0%

	PAYMENT	INTEREST			
YEAR	AMOUNT	6%	8%	10%	12%
0	$1,000	$ 943	$ 926	$ 909	$ 893
5	1,000	4,212	3,993	3,791	3,605
10	1,000	7,360	6,710	6,145	5,650
15	1,000	9,712	8,559	7,606	6,811
20	1,000	11,470	9,818	8,514	7,469
25	1,000	12,783	10,675	9,077	7,843
30	1,000	13,765	11,258	9,427	8,055

TABLE 2

ESCALATION RATE 4%

YEARS	PAYMENT AMOUNT	INTEREST 6%	8%	10%	12%
0	$1,000	$ 943	$ 926	$ 909	$ 893
5	1,217	4,542	4,299	4,076	3,870
10	1,480	8,672	7,859	7,155	6,543
15	1,801	12,426	10,807	9,481	8,387
20	2,191	15,840	13,247	11,238	9,661
25	2,665	18,840	15,268	12,566	10,540
30	3,243	21,765	16,942	13,569	11,467

TABLE 3

ESCALATION RATE 5%

YEARS	PAYMENT AMOUNT	INTEREST 6%	8%	10%	12%
0	$1,000	$ 943	$ 926	$ 909	$ 893
5	1,276	4,629	4,379	4,151	3,940
10	1,629	9,043	8,184	7,440	6,793
15	2,079	13,254	11,488	10,046	8,860
20	2,653	17,269	14,358	12,112	10,356
25	3,386	21,098	16,851	13,749	11,440
30	4,322	24,751	19,017	15,046	12,225

TABLE 4

ESCALATION RATE 6%

YEARS	PAYMENT AMOUNT	INTEREST 6%	8%	10%	12%
0	$1,000	$ 943	$ 926	$ 909	$ 893
5	1,338	4,717	4,461	4,227	4,011
10	1,791	9,434	8,525	7,739	7,057
15	2,397	14,151	12,225	10,657	9,369
20	3,207	18,868	15,596	13,082	11,125
25	4,292	23,586	18,666	15,097	12,459
30	5,743	28,302	21,461	16,771	13,472

TABLE 5

ESCALATION RATE 7%

YEAR	PAYMENT AMOUNT	6%	INTEREST 8%	10%	12%
0	$1,000	$ 943	$ 926	$ 909	$ 893
5	1,405	4,807	4,545	4,304	4,083
10	1,967	9,845	8,883	8,053	7,333
15	2,759	15,125	13,024	11,317	9,919
20	3,870	20,659	16,977	14,160	11,977
25	5,427	26,458	20,750	16,636	13,615
30	7,612	32,537	24,351	18,792	14,918

TABLE 6

ESCALATION RATE 8%

YEARS	PAYMENT AMOUNT	6%	INTEREST 8%	10%	12%
0	$1,000	$ 943	$ 926	$ 909	$ 893
5	1,469	4,898	4,630	4,383	4,157
10	2,159	10,277	9,259	8,382	7,622
15	3,172	16,182	13,889	12,030	10,511
20	4,661	22,665	18,519	15,359	12,920
25	6,848	29,784	23,148	18,396	14,929
30	10,063	37,601	27,778	21,166	16,603

TABLE 7

ESCALATION RATE 9%

YEAR	PAYMENT AMOUNT	6%	INTEREST 8%	10%	12%
0	$1,000	$ 943	$ 926	$ 909	$ 893
5	1,539	4,992	4,716	4,464	4,231
10	2,367	10,731	9,655	8,728	7,926
15	3,642	17,329	14,826	12,802	11,151
20	5,604	24,916	20,242	16,694	13,967
25	8,623	33,639	25,912	20,412	16,425
30	13,268	43,668	31,851	23,965	18,572

TABLE 8

ESCALATION RATE 10%

YEARS	PAYMENT AMOUNT	INTEREST 6%	8%	10%	12%
0	$1,000	$ 943	$ 926	$ 909	$ 893
5	1,611	5,086	4,804	4,545	4,308
10	2,594	11,208	10,070	9,091	8,244
15	4,177	18,576	15,842	13,636	11,842
20	6,728	27,442	22,169	18,182	15,129
25	10,835	38,112	29,103	22,727	18,133
30	17,449	50,953	36,704	27,273	20,879

APPENDIX B

HISTORICAL FINANCIAL DATA

APPENDIX B-1   212

    HISTORICAL INFLATION RATES
    PURCHASING POWER OF THE DOLLAR

APPENDIX B-2   213

    HISTORICAL INTEREST RATES

APPENDIX B-3   214

    HISTORICAL RETURN ON STOCKS

APPENDIX B-1

HISTORIC INFLATION RATES

YEAR	PRODUCER PRICES	ANNUAL INCREASE	CONSUMER PRICES	ANNUAL INCREASE
1951	3.247	8.43	3.846	7.35
1952	3.268	-0.65	3.765	2.11
1953	3.300	-0.98	3.735	0.80
1954	3.289	0.33	3.717	0.48
1955	3.279	0.30	3.732	-0.40
1956	3.195	2.56	3.678	1.45
1957	3.077	3.69	3.549	3.51
1958	3.012	2.11	3.457	2.59
1959	3.021	-0.30	3.427	0.87
1960	2.994	0.89	3.373	1.58
1961	2.994	0.00	3.340	0.98
1962	2.985	0.30	3.304	1.08
1963	2.994	-0.30	3.265	1.18
1964	2.985	0.30	3.220	1.38
1965	2.933	1.74	3.166	1.68
1966	2.841	3.14	3.080	2.72
1967	2.809	1.13	2.993	2.82
1968	2.732	2.74	2.873	4.01
1969	2.632	3.66	2.726	5.12
1970	2.545	3.31	2.574	5.58
1971	2.469	2.99	2.466	4.20
1972	2.392	3.12	2.391	3.04
1973	2.193	8.32	2.251	5.86
1974	1.901	13.32	2.029	9.86
1975	1.718	9.63	1.859	8.38
1976	1.645	4.25	1.757	5.49
1977	1.546	6.02	1.649	6.15
1978	1.433	7.31	1.532	7.10
1979	1.289	10.05	1.380	9.92
1980	1.136	11.87	1.215	11.96
1981	1.041	8.36	1.098	9.63
1982	1.000	3.94	1.035	5.74
1983	0.984	1.60	1.003	3.09
1984	0.964	2.03	0.961	4.19
1985	0.955	0.93	0.928	3.43
1986	0.969	-1.47	0.913	1.62
1987	0.949	2.06	0.880	3.61
1988	0.926	2.42	0.846	3.86
1989			0.812	4.02
1990			0.770	5.17

Source: U.S Bureau of Labor Statistics

APPENDIX B-2
HISTORIC INTEREST RATES

YEAR	MUNI. BONDS AAA	LG.TM. CORP. AAA	LG.TM. GOV'T BONDS	PREFERED STOCK YIELDS
1952	2.19	2.87	2.68	4.13
1953	2.72	3.08	2.90	4.27
1954	2.73	2.74	2.52	4.02
1955	2.53	2.97	2.80	4.01
1956	2.93	3.34	3.06	4.25
1957	3.60	3.80	3.47	4.63
1958	3.56	3.65	3.23	4.45
1959	3.95	4.25	4.10	4.69
1960	3.73	4.26	3.99	4.75
1961	3.46	4.20	3.90	4.66
1962	3.18	4.18	3.95	4.50
1963	3.23	4.13	4.02	4.30
1964	3.22	4.26	4.17	4.32
1965	3.27	4.39	4.23	4.33
1966	3.82	5.09	4.68	4.97
1967	3.98	5.47	4.90	5.34
1968	4.51	6.12	5.33	5.78
1969	5.81	6.92	6.22	6.41
1970	6.51	7.76	6.75	7.22
1971	5.70	7.16	5.94	6.75
1972	5.27	7.09	5.67	7.27
1973	5.18	7.37	6.12	7.23
1974	6.09	8.04	6.59	8.23
1975	6.89	8.43	8.21	8.38
1976	6.49	8.21	7.87	7.97
1977	5.56	8.10	7.69	7.60
1978	5.90	8.65	8.46	8.25
1979	6.39	9.43	9.27	9.07
1980	8.51	11.56	11.22	10.57
1981	11.23	13.72	13.20	12.38
1982	11.57	13.03	12.51	12.53
1983	9.47	11.45	11.09	11.02
1984	10.15	12.43	12.34	11.59
1985	9.18	10.94	10.74	10.44
1986	7.38	9.02	8.14	8.76
1987	7.73	9.32	8.76	8.37
1988	7.76	9.55	9.11	9.23
1989	7.24	9.16	8.62	9.04
1990	7.04	9.03E	8.38	8.72
1991	6.63	8.24	7.62	8.24

APPENDIX B-3

HISTORIC RETURN ON STOCKS
S&P 500

YEAR	PRICE INDEX	PERCENT ANNUAL CHANGE	PERCENT ANNUAL DIVIDEND	TOTAL RETURN PERCENT
1954	29.7	16.71	4.95	21.66
1955	40.5	26.67	4.08	30.75
1956	46.6	13.15	4.09	17.24
1957	44.4	-5.05	4.35	-0.70
1958	46.2	4.02	3.97	7.99
1959	57.4	19.41	3.23	22.64
1960	55.9	-2.74	3.47	0.73
1961	68.3	18.19	2.98	21.17
1962	66.3	-3.02	3.37	0.35
1963	69.9	5.15	3.17	8.32
1964	81.4	14.13	3.01	17.14
1965	88.2	7.71	3.00	10.71
1966	85.3	-3.41	3.40	-0.01
1967	91.9	7.26	3.20	10.46
1968	98.7	6.85	3.07	9.92
1969	97.8	-0.87	3.24	2.37
1970	83.2	-17.57	3.83	-13.74
1971	98.3	15.33	3.14	18.47
1972	109.2	9.99	2.84	12.83
1973	107.4	-1.68	3.06	1.38
1974	82.8	-29.63	4.47	-25.16
1975	86.2	3.84	4.31	8.15
1976	102.0	15.53	3.77	19.30
1977	98.2	-3.87	4.62	0.75
1978	96.0	-2.27	5.28	3.01
1979	103.0	6.78	5.47	12.25
1980	118.8	13.30	5.26	18.56
1981	128.1	7.26	5.20	12.46
1982	119.7	-7.02	5.81	-1.21
1983	160.4	25.37	4.40	29.77
1984	160.5	0.06	4.64	4.70
1985	186.8	14.08	4.25	18.33
1986	236.3	20.95	3.49	24.44
1987	286.8	17.61	3.08	20.69
1988	265.8	-7.90	3.64	-4.26
1989	322.8	17.66	3.13	21.11
1990	330.2	2.29	3.66	5.95

APPENDIX C

MISCELLANEOUS ATTACHMENTS

APPENDIX C-1   216

    LIFE EXPECTANCY IN THE
    UNITED STATES

APPENDIX C-2   217

    JOINT LIFE AND LAST
    SURVIVOR LIFE EXPECTANCY

APPENDIX C-3   218

    LIFE EXPECTANCY TABLES
    FOR ANNUITIES

APPENDIX C-4   219

    1986 TAX SCHEDULE
    (10-YEAR AVERAGING)

APPENDIX C-5   220

    10-YEAR AVERAGING TAX TABLE

APPENDIX C-6   221
    VALUE OF WAITING TO DRAW
    SOCIAL SECURITY

APPENDIX C-1

UNITED STATES LIFE EXPECTANCY

AGE IN 1986	TOTAL	WHITE MALE	WHITE FEMALE	BLACK MALE	BLACK FEMALE
40	37.4	34.9	40.5	30.3	36.6
41	36.5	34.0	39.6	29.5	35.7
42	35.6	33.1	38.6	28.7	34.8
43	34.7	32.2	37.7	28.0	34.0
44	33.8	31.3	36.7	27.2	33.1
45	32.9	30.4	35.8	26.4	32.2
46	32.0	29.5	34.9	25.7	31.4
47	31.1	28.7	33.9	24.9	30.5
48	30.2	27.8	33.0	24.1	29.7
49	29.4	26.9	32.1	23.4	26.8
50	28.5	26.1	31.2	22.7	28.0
51	27.6	25.2	30.3	22.0	27.2
52	26.8	24.4	29.4	21.3	26.4
53	26.0	23.6	28.6	20.6	25.6
54	25.1	22.7	27.7	19.9	24.8
55	24.3	21.9	26.8	19.3	24.0
56	23.5	21.2	26.0	18.6	23.3
57	22.7	20.4	25.1	18.0	22.5
58	21.9	19.6	24.3	17.3	21.8
59	21.2	18.9	23.4	16.7	21.0
60	20.4	18.2	22.6	16.1	20.3
61	19.7	17.5	21.8	15.5	19.6
62	18.9	16.8	21.0	15.0	19.0
63	18.2	16.1	20.2	14.4	18.3
64	17.5	15.4	19.5	13.9	17.7
65	16.8	14.8	18.7	13.4	17.0
70	13.6	11.7	15.1	10.8	13.9
75	10.7	9.1	11.8	8.7	11.1
80	8.1	6.9	8.8	6.8	8.5
85 and over	6.0	5.1	6.4	5.5	6.7

SOURCE: BUREAU OF LABOR STATISTICS
(1991 ANNUAL)

APPENDIX C-2

JOINT AND LAST SURVIVOR

LIFE EXPECTANCY

AGES	55	56	57	58	59	60	61	62	63	64	65
55	34.4	33.9	33.5	33.1	32.7	32.3	32.0	31.7	31.4	31.1	30.9
56	33.9	33.4	33.0	32.5	32.1	31.7	31.4	31.0	30.7	30.4	30.2
57	33.5	33.0	32.5	32.0	31.6	31.2	30.8	30.4	30.1	29.8	29.5
58	33.1	32.5	32.0	31.5	31.1	30.6	30.2	29.9	29.5	29.2	28.9
59	32.7	32.1	31.6	31.1	30.6	30.1	29.7	29.3	28.9	28.6	28.2
60	32.3	31.7	31.2	30.6	30.1	29.7	29.2	28.8	28.4	28.0	27.6
61	32.0	31.4	30.8	30.2	29.7	29.2	28.7	28.3	27.8	27.4	27.1
62	31.7	31.0	30.4	29.9	29.3	28.8	28.3	27.8	27.3	26.9	26.5
63	31.4	30.7	30.1	29.5	28.9	28.4	27.8	27.3	26.9	26.4	26.0
64	31.1	30.4	29.8	29.2	28.6	28.0	27.4	26.9	26.4	25.9	25.5
65	30.9	30.2	29.5	28.9	28.2	27.6	27.1	26.5	26.0	25.5	25.0
66	30.6	29.6	29.2	28.6	27.9	27.3	26.7	26.1	25.6	25.1	24.6
67	30.4	29.7	29.0	28.3	27.6	27.0	26.4	25.8	25.2	24.7	24.2
68	30.2	29.5	28.8	28.1	27.4	26.7	26.1	25.5	24.9	24.3	23.8
69	30.1	29.3	28.6	27.8	27.1	26.5	25.8	25.2	24.6	24.0	23.4
70	29.9	29.1	28.4	27.6	26.9	26.2	25.6	24.9	24.3	23.7	23.1
71	29.7	29.0	28.2	27.5	26.7	26.0	25.3	24.7	24.0	23.4	22.8
72	29.6	28.8	28.1	27.3	26.5	25.8	25.1	24.4	23.8	23.1	22.5
73	29.5	28.7	27.9	27.1	26.4	25.6	24.9	24.2	23.5	22.9	22.2
74	29.4	28.6	27.8	27.0	26.2	25.5	24.7	24.0	23.3	22.7	22.0
75	29.3	28.5	27.7	26.9	26.1	25.3	24.6	23.8	23.1	22.4	21.8

AGES	66	67	68	69	70	71	72	73	74	75
66	24.1	23.7	23.3	22.9	22.5	22.2	21.9	21.6	21.4	21.1
67	23.7	23.2	22.8	22.4	22.0	21.7	21.3	21.0	20.8	20.5
68	23.3	22.8	22.3	21.9	21.5	21.2	20.8	20.5	20.2	19.9
69	22.9	22.4	21.9	21.5	21.1	20.7	20.3	20.0	19.6	19.3
70	22.5	22.0	21.5	21.1	20.6	20.2	19.8	19.4	19.1	18.8
71	22.2	21.7	21.2	20.7	20.2	19.8	19.4	19.0	18.6	18.3
72	21.9	21.3	20.8	20.3	19.8	19.4	18.9	18.5	18.2	17.8
73	21.6	21.0	20.5	20.0	19.4	19.0	18.5	18.1	17.7	17.3
74	21.4	20.8	20.2	19.6	19.1	18.6	18.2	17.7	17.3	16.9
75	21.1	20.5	19.9	19.3	18.8	18.3	17.8	17.3	16.9	16.5

SOURCE: IRS PUBLICATION 939

APPENDIX C-3

LIFE EXPECTANCY TABLES

FOR ANNUITY TAXES

AGES MALE	FEMALE	BEFORE 7/1/86 MULTIPLES	AGE UNISEX	AFTER 7/1/86 MULTIPLES
45	50	29.6	45	37.7
46	51	28.7	46	36.8
47	52	27.9	47	35.9
48	53	27.1	48	34.9
49	54	26.3	49	34.0
50	55	25.5	50	33.1
51	56	24.7	51	32.2
52	57	24.0	52	31.3
53	58	23.2	53	30.4
54	59	22.4	54	29.5
55	60	21.7	55	28.6
56	61	21.0	56	27.7
57	62	20.3	57	26.8
58	63	19.6	58	25.9
59	64	18.9	59	25.0
60	65	18.2	60	24.2
61	66	17.5	61	23.3
62	67	16.9	62	22.5
63	68	16.2	63	21.6
64	69	15.6	64	20.8
65	70	15.0	65	20.0
66	71	14.4	66	19.2
67	72	13.8	67	18.4
68	73	13.2	68	17.6
69	74	12.6	69	16.8
70	75	12.1	70	16.0
71	76	11.6	71	15.3
72	77	11.0	72	14.6
73	78	10.5	73	13.9
74	79	10.1	74	13.2
75	80	9.6	75	12.5

SOURCE: IRS PUBLICATION 939

APPENDIX C-4

1986 TAX SCHEDULE

SINGLE TAXPAYERS

TABLE FOR CALCULATION OF TAXES
10 YEAR AVERAGING.

TAXABLE INCOME			PLUS	AMOUNT
OVER	NOT OVER	TAX IS	%	OVER
0	2,480	0.00	0	
2,480	3,670	0.00	11	2,480
3,670	4,750	130.90	12	3,670
4,750	7,010	260.50	14	4,750
7,010	9,170	576.90	15	7,010
9,170	11,650	900.90	16	9,170
11,650	13,920	1,297.70	18	11,650
13,920	16,190	1,706.30	20	13,920
16,190	19,640	2,160.30	23	16,190
19,640	25,360	2,953.80	26	19,640
25,360	31,080	4,441.00	30	25,360
31,080	36,800	6,157.00	34	31,080
36,800	44,780	8,101.80	38	36,800
44,780	59,670	11,134.20	42	44,780
59,670	88,270	17,388.00	48	59,670
88,270		31,116.00	50	88,270

APPENDIX C-5

10-YEAR AVERAGING TAX TABLE

TAXES ON LUMP–SUM 10 YEAR AVERAGING

AT LEAST	NOT OVER	TAX	PLUS THIS %	OVER
	$20,000	0	5.5	0
$20,000	21,583	$1,100	13.2	$20,000
21,583	30,583	1,309	14.4	21,583
30,583	49,417	2,605	16.8	30,583
49,417	67,417	5,769	18.0	49,417
67,417	70,000	9,009	19.2	67,417
70,000	91,700	9,505	16.0	70,000
91,700	114,400	12,977	18.0	91,700
114,400	137,100	17,063	20.0	114,400
137,100	171,600	21,603	23.0	137,100
171,600	228,800	29,538	26.0	171,600
228,800	286,000	44,410	30.0	228,800
286,000	343,200	61,570	34.0	286,000
343,200	423,000	81,018	38.0	343,200
423,000	571,900	111,342	42.0	423,000
571,900	857,900	173,880	48.0	571,900
857,900		311,160	50.0	857,90

APPENDIX C-6
VALUE OF WAITING TO START SOCIAL
SECURITY PAYMENTS

```
BASIS:
  HUSBAND AND WIFE ARE SAME AGE, 62 IN
    1992 SPOUSE HAS NOT WORKED
  AT 62 YEARS OF AGE INSURED DRAWS 80%
    OF PIA, SPOUSE DRAWS 37.5% OF PIA
  AT AGE 65 INSURED DRAWS 100% OF PIA
    SPOUSE DRAWS 50% OF PIA
  PIA          $1022 PER MONTH
  PAYMENTS INFLATED    4% PER YEAR
```

	ANNUAL	PAYMENT	DIFF	PERCENT	NPV
YEAR	AGE 65	AGE 62	65-62	INTEREST	(10%)
1	0	13490	-13490	%	-12264
2	0	14030	-14030		-23859
3	0	14591	-14591		-34821
4	19897	15174	4722	-75.05	-31596
5	20693	15781	4911	-46.48	-28546
6	21520	16413	5107	-29.52	-25663
7	22381	17069	5311	-18.71	-22937
8	23276	17752	5524	-11.37	-20360
9	24207	18462	5745	-6.16	-17924
10	25176	19201	5975	-2.32	-15620
11	26183	19969	6214	0.58	-13442
12	27230	20767	6462	2.82	-11383
13	28319	21598	6721	4.59	-9436
14	29452	22462	6990	6.00	-7595
15	30630	23361	7269	7.15	-5855
16	31855	24295	7560	8.09	-4209
17	33130	25267	7862	8.88	-2654
18	34455	26277	8177	9.53	-1183
19	35833	27329	8504	10.08	206
20	37266	28422	8844	10.54	1521
21	38757	29559	9198	10.94	2764
22	40307	30741	9566	11.29	3939
23	41920	31971	9949	11.58	5050
24	43597	33250	10347	11.84	6101
25	45340	34580	10760	12.06	7094
26	47154	35963	11191	12.25	8033
27	49040	37401	11639	12.42	8921
28	51002	38897	12104	12.57	9760
29	53042	40453	12588	12.70	10554
30	55164	42071	13092	12.82	11304

APPENDIX D

FINANCIAL EXAMPLES

APPENDIX D-1   224

   BALANCING INCOME AND EXPENSES

APPENDIX D-2   239

   ESTIMATING SOCIAL SECURITY
   BENEFITS

APPENDIX D-3   248

   INSURANCE CALCULATIONS

APPENDIX D-1

BALANCING INCOME AND EXPENSES

OTHER EXAMPLES FROM CHAPTER 5

CHAPTER 5 (BALANCING INCOME AND EXPENSES) gave 2 examples on how to calculate the amount of total earning assets (including Social Security and other fixed income) that is required at the beginning of retirement to maintain a given standard of living. The examples given below are additional examples relating to that chapter.

EXAMPLE 3

Mr. and Mrs. Jones feel they need living expenses of $40,000 per year, based on their 1992 expenditures. They are both 65 years of age, but both are very healthy and do not smoke, so they took 30 years as their life expectancy. They will draw Social Security of $15,000 per year in 1992. They have a nest egg of $500,000 that has been earning 8% interest per year. They have no other income. They would like to know how much more money they need to live out their life with their current standard of living. Assume an inflation rate of 4% per year.

In contrast to Example 2, Chapter 5, all factors increase according to the inflation rate, so the withdrawals from savings also will increase at the inflation rate.

At 8% interest and an inflation rate of 4%, $1,000 per year requires an initial sum of $16,942. Dividing this $16,942 into the $500,000 we get a figure of 29,512. Thus, the first year's withdrawal could be as high as $29,512. This figure will escalate at 4% per year reaching $95,719 in 30 years when the amount in the kitty will reach zero.

The table given below is similar to that of Example 2 except that incomes and expenses are used instead of total assets.

	YEAR	
	1992	2122
NEED	$40,000	$129,736
SOCIAL SECURITY	$15,000	48,651
REQUIRED FROM SAVINGS	25,000	81,085
AVAILABLE FROM SAVINGS	29,512	95,719

The required amount is less than that available, so they have some money to spare and should get along quite well.

EXAMPLE 4

Take a case identical to Example 3 except that the nest egg is $300,000. The Joneses would like to know how much more of a retirement sum they will need to retire at their same standard of living.

From TABLE 2, APPENDIX A-5 at 4% inflation and 8% interest we get the

figure, $16,942, that give an inflated
$1,000 a year over the thirty years.
Dividing this into $300,000 gives a
figure of 17.71. Thus, they can take out
$17,710 a year in the first year and
inflate the withdrawals by 4% per year.
Their first and last year of the 30-year
plan would look like this:

	YEAR	
	1992	2122
NEED	$40,000	$129,736
SOCIAL		
SECURITY	$15,000	48,651
REQUIRED FROM		
SAVINGS	25,000	81,085
AVAILABLE FROM		
SAVINGS	17,710	57,432
SHORTFALL	7,290	23,653

In this example, they must handle
the deficiency by either reducing
spending, or by having more money at the
beginning of retirement. At the same 4%
inflation and 8% return on investment the
extra money they will require is
$7,290/$1,000 x $16,942 or $123,507.

Using this example but with 10%
return on money, TABLE 2, APPENDIX A-5,
gives $13,564 per $1,000 of initial
income. The initial withdrawal from the
$300,000 is calculated as follows:

(300,000/13,564) x $1,000 = $22,117

The shortfall in the first year
would be $2,883 a year. The extra money
required at 10% interest is:

2.883 X $13,564 or $39,105.

EXAMPLE 5

Mr. and Mrs. White are 65 and 57 years of age respectively. Mrs. White is a homemaker and has not developed Social Security eligibility. They have an income need of $30,000 a year in current dollars. Mr. White is drawing Social Security payments of $9,000 a year. Mrs. White will be eligible for 37.5% of his Social Security payments in 5 years. Mr. White is also drawing a company pension of $10,000 a year, escalating at the inflation rate. Using an assumption of 4% inflation and 8% interest on savings, they would like to know how much money they should have in their savings. The table below was set up to show the figures at the essential dates.

	1992	1997	2022
NEED	30,000	44,407	97,302
SOCIAL SECURITY	9,000	15,056	40,137
PENSION	10,000	12,167	32,435
PENSION PLUS SOC.SEC.	19,000	27,223	72,572
FROM SAVINGS (BY DIFFERENCE)	11,000	17,184	24,730

The Social Security figure in 1997 was calculated by escalating the $9,000 figure by 4% per year for 5 years, and then adding the wife's 37.5% which begins in 1997.

$$(\$9,000 \times (1.04)^5) \times 1.375 = \$15,056$$

The lump-sum required from savings in 1992 is solved by breaking the 30 year period into a first 5-year period and then, a second 25-year period.

5 YEAR PERIOD CALCULATION

The figure of $4,299 is found in TABLE 2, APPENDIX A-5 (5 years, 4% inflation, 8% interest). The lump-sum required to fund this 5 year period is:

$11,000 x (4,299/1,000) = $47,289.

25 YEAR PERIOD CALCULATION

Again, from TABLE 2, APPENDIX A-5, (25 years, 4% inflation, 8% interest) we get $15,268. The initial need in 1997 is $17,184. The sum needed in 1997 is accordingly:

$17,184 x (15,268/1,000) = $262,365.

We must adjust this figure for the interest that would be earned in the five years between 1992 and 1997. At 8% per year compounded annually, a factor of 1.469 is found in APPENDIX A-2 $(1.08)^5$. The sum needed in 1992 for this second period is then $262,365/1.469 or $178,601.

The total sum needed by the Whites is $178,601 + 47,289 or $225,890

EXAMPLE 6

The same data of Example 5 is used in the alternate method of calculation. The table of Example 5 is repeated below:

	1992	1997	2022
NEED	30,000	44,407	97,302
SOCIAL SECURITY	9,000	15,056	40,137
PENSION	10,000	12,167	32,435
PENSION PLUS SOC.SEC.	19,000	27,223	72,572
FROM SAVINGS (BY DIFFERENCE)	11,000	17,184	24,730

The same procedure of Example 2 is used except it is divided into a five-year period and a 25-year period.

5 YEAR CALCULATION

		ESCALATION %	FACTOR	SUM
1992 NEED	$30,000	4	4,299	$128,970
SOCIAL SECURITY	9,000	4	4,299	38,691
PENSION	10,000	4	4,299	42,990
FROM SAVINGS (BY DIFFERENCE)	11,000			47,289

The sum of $47,289, the amount needed for the first 5-year period, is identical with the figure in example 5.

25 YEAR CALCULATION

		ESCALATION %	FACTOR	SUM
1997 NEED	44,407	4	15,268	678,006
SOCIAL SECURITY	15,056	4	15,268	229,875
PENSION	12,167	4	15,268	185,766
FROM SAVINGS (BY DIFFERENCE)	17,184	4	15,268	262,365

Again as in Example 5 we must adjust for the five years of interest before this date.

$$\text{Amount } 1992 = \text{Amount } 1997/(1.08)^5$$
$$= 262,365/1.469$$
$$= \$178,601$$

The total amount required at the time of retirement is the sum of the amounts needed for each period.

$$\$178,601 + 47,289 = \$225,890$$
This amount is identical with that calculated in example 5.

COMPARISON OF EXAMPLES

The six examples (here and from Chapter 5) represent a range of cases. They all show a need increasing with inflation. Your case may show a need with discontinuities due to such factors as a spouse working longer than the principal income earner, or a home paid off. You may have discontinuities in income earning assets due to situations such as sale of business or annuity payments beginning or ending.

Just remember the terms "Estimation" and "Approximation." The future is murky at best. The word "Judgment" is important. You must understand your position sufficiently to make good decisions.

TAXES AND NEEDS

Up to now the examples have assumed taxes increased constantly with inflation. Chapter 10 covers special taxes you might have at retirement. You should consider the effect of taxes on your withdrawals. We will be risky and assume the tax structure in effect today will be in effect long range. For purposes here we will use 1991 taxes and information.

EXAMPLE 7

Mr. and Mrs. Black have a 1992 need of $40,000 a year before taxes. Their income will be from Social Security ($12,000 a year), a company pension ($18,000 a year), and the balance from savings. They pay alimony of $2400 a year, property taxes of $1,000 a year, charity of $1,000 a year, and have mortgage interest of $2,500 a year. The pension is fixed and does not escalate with inflation.

Their savings may have different possibilities as follows:

7-A   The Blacks have $200,000 in a tax deferred 401(k) plan. Tax is only on the part withdrawn each year.

7-B   The $200,000 is divided equally with $100,000 in a tax deferred IRA, and $100,000 in certificates of deposit purchased with money that has already been taxed. They will deplete the C.D.s first, but must pay taxes on their income each year. Withdrawals from the C.D. principal are not taxed.

7-C   The $200,000 is all in certificates of deposit from money that has already been taxed. All income from

this will be taxed, but the
principal will not be taxed.

7-D   The $200,000 is in a variable
       annuity that pays out for 25 years
       starting when they are age 65. They
       purchased the annuity for a total
       sum of $100,000. Since it is a
       variable annuity, with payments
       increasing 4% per year, and since
       they made some payments after June
       30, 1986, special rules apply.
       Because of these caveats, the unisex
       table of APPENDIX C-2 is used to get
       the years over which their
       contributions can be deducted from
       taxable income. A figure of 20
       years is given, which means they can
       deduct $5,000 a year from the normal
       taxable amount ($100,000/20). The
       first year's payment is $13,099.

       A table can be set up to calculate
how much must be withdrawn from the four
plans to cover the needs and taxes. The
detailed calculations are given in TABLE
1 D-1, (at the end of this section) for
the first year that is summarized below.

CASE	7-A	7-B	7-C	7-D
NEED				
LESS TAX	$40,000	$40,000	$40,000	$40,000
STATE TAX	1,242	636	1,196	643
FEDERAL TAX	3,333	2,125	3,631	2,138
TOTAL NEED	44,575	42,761	44,827	42,781
INCOME				
FROM SOC.SEC	12,000	12,000	12,000	12,000
FROM PENSION	18,000	18,000	18,000	18,000
FROM 401K	14,575	0	0	0
FROM OTHER		12,761	14,827	13,099
TOTAL INCOME	44,575	42,761	44,827	43,099
TAXED INTEREST	0	8,000	16,000	8,099
TAXED SOC.SEC.	2,088	0	2,800	0
GROSS INCOME	34,633	26,000	36,800	26,099
TAXED INCOME	22,221	14,164	24,208	14,256

The picture we have painted above gives a very poor story of the long-term assessment on how the money will last. For example, Case 7-C is the most favorable of the situations, but shows the highest withdrawal in the first year. To get an exact solution of the spending that could be supported, a year-by-year analysis for the 25 years would be required. The effort would be very high and the answers subject to the uncertainties of the future.

We simplify the calculations by converting all cases to single premium annuities, in which a variable benefit is paid that escalates at 4% a year. The tax laws allow a fixed amount per year to be exempt from taxes, depending on age and the amount of money paid that has already been taxed. (See 7-D above). These changes make it possible to get the asset value of the components of the needs and sources of income. The results will certainly be different from the year by year calculations, but the calculations can be done without a large effort. This should not be taken as an endorsement of annuities.

Since the savings are converted to annuities, the amount withdrawn each year is fixed for all cases, but the tax situation is different because of the nature of the savings. The withdrawals from tax deferred savings will have a higher tax than withdrawals from a savings of already taxed money. One can find the taxes for the various cases in TABLE 2 D-1 (at the end of this section), which is the detailed calculation sheet. Since taxes are dependent on the annuity benefit, which escalates at 4% per year, the taxes are assumed to escalate at the same rate. The total initial requirement will then be the amount for the need before taxes plus the amount for taxes.

All cases assume 8% interest on the money and a 25-year pay out period. An escalation of 4% per year was assumed for all but the pension, which does not escalate. The initial available amount is the same for all situations.

AVAILABLE ASSETS

FROM SOCIAL SECURITY
     $12,000/yr x 15.268   = $183,216
FROM PENSION
     $18,000/yr x 10.675   = $192,150
FROM SAVINGS $200,000
     TOTAL ASSETS $575,366

The lump sum need before taxes is given below for three levels of annual need.

ANNUAL NEED			TOTAL AMOUNT
$40,000	x 15.268 =		$610,720
35,000	x 15.268 =		$534,380
30,000	x 15.268 =		$458,040

CALCULATION OF TOTAL NEED

LUMP-SUM NEEDED TO PAY TAXES

	7-A	7-B	7-C	7-D
TAXES/YR	$4,111	$2,781	$1,730	$2,781
LUMP-SUM	$62,767	$42,460	$26,414	$42,460

TOTAL (NEED BEFORE TAXES PLUS TAXES)

$40,000	$673,487	$653,180	$637,134	$653,180
35,000	597,147	576,840	560,794	576,840
30,000	520,807	500,500	484,454	500,500

RETIREMENT GAP

ANNUAL NEED	GAP, DOLLARS			
$40,000	-$98,121	-$77,814	-$61,768	-$77,814
35,000	-$21,781	-$ 1,474	$14,572	-$ 1,474
30,000	$54,559	$74,866	$90,912	$74,866

The difference in gap between the nest egg from already taxed money and one that is totally tax deferred is $36,353. For this case a tax deferred savings of $236,353 is equivalent to $200,000 of savings from taxed funds.

If the money is to last for 25 years, the Blacks must reduce their spending from $40,000 a year to the values below, depending on the savings tax status. These figures were determined by interpolation of the values for the retirement gap.

```
         Case 7-A        $33,500 per year
              7-B         34,900
              7-C         36,000
              7-D         34,900
```

TABLE 2 D-1, shows that more money
is withdrawn from savings in early years
than needed. This money must be set
aside for later years when the need will
exceed the income.

TABLE 1 D-1

CALCULATION OF FIRST YEAR TAXES

NEED	7-A	7-B	7-C	7-D
LESS TAX	40,000	40,000	40,000	40,000
STATE TAX	1,242	636	1,196	643
FEDERAL TAX	3,333	2,125	3,631	2,138
TOTAL NEED	44,575	42,761	44,827	42,781
INCOME				
FROM SOC.SEC	12,000	12,000	12,000	12,000
FROM PENSION	18,000	18,000	18,000	18,000
FROM 401K	14,575	0	0	0
FROM OTHER		12,761	14,827	13,099
TOTAL INCOME	44,575	42,761	44,827	43,099
TAXED INTEREST	0	8,000	16,000	8,099

CALCULATION OF OF SOCIAL SECURITY TO BE TAXED				
INCOME	32,575	26,000	34,000	26,099
ALIMONY	2,400	2,400	2,400	2,400
TOTAL ADJ. INC.	30,175	23,600	31,600	23,699
50 % SOC SEC	6,000	6,000	6,000	6,000
TOTAL	36,175	29,600	37,600	29,699
LESS BASE	32,000	32,000	32,000	32,000
DIFFERENCE	4,175	(2,400)	5,600	(2,301)
TAXABLE S.S.	2,088	0	2,800	0

CALCULATION OF TAXABLE INCOME				
GROSS INCOME	34,663	26,000	36,800	26,099
PROPERTY TAX	1,000	1,000	1,000	1,000
MORT.INTEREST	2,500	2,500	2,500	2,500
STATE TAXES	1,242	636	1,392	643
EXEMPTIONS	4,300	4,300	4,300	4,300
CHARITY	1,000	1,000	1,000	1,000
TOTAL DEDUCTION	10,042	9,436	10,192	9,443
ADJUSTMENT	2,400	2,400	2,400	2,400
TAXED INCOME	22,221	14,164	24,208	14,256

TABLE 2 D-1
LONG TERM RETIREMENT TAXES
ALL SAVINGS CONVERTED TO AN EQUIVALENT VARIABLE ANNUITY

	7-A	7-B	7-C	7-D
NEED				
LESS TAX	40,000	40,000	40,000	40,000
STATE TAX	1,087	643	288	643
FEDERAL TAX	3,024	2,138	1,442	2,138
TOTAL NEED	44,111	42,781	41,730	42,781
INCOME				
FROM SOC.SEC	12,000	12,000	12,000	12,000
FROM PENSION	18,000	18,000	18,000	18,000
FROM 401K	13,099	0	0	0
FROM OTHER	0	13,099	13,099	13,099
TOTAL INCOME	43,099	43,099	43,099	43,099
TAXED INCOME	13,099	8,099	3,099	8,099
CALCULATION OF SOCIAL SECURITY TO BE TAXED				
INCOME	31,099	26,099	21,099	26,099
ALIMONY	2,400	2,400	2,400	2,400
TOTAL ADJ. INC.	28,699	23,699	18,699	23,699
50 % SOC SEC	6,000	6,000	6,000	6,000
TOTAL	34,699	29,699	24,699	29,699
LESS BASE	32,000	32,000	32,000	32,000
DIFFERENCE	2,699	(2,301)	(7,301)	(2,301)
TAXABLE S.S.	1,350	0	0	0
CALCULATION OF TAXABLE INCOME				
GROSS INCOME	32,449	26,099	21,099	26,099
PROPERTY TAX	1,000	1,000	1,000	1,000
MORT.INTEREST	2,500	2,500	2,500	2,500
STATE TAXES	1,087	643	288	643
EXEMPTIONS	4,300	4,300	4,300	4,300
CHARITY	1,000	1,000	1,000	1,000
TOTAL DEDUCTION	9,887	9,443	9,088	9,443
ADJUSTMENT	2,400	2,400	2,400	2,400
TAXED INCOME	20,161	14,256	9,611	14,256
FEDERAL TAXES				
1ST TIER	3,024	2,138	1,442	2,138
2ND TIER				
TOTAL	3,024	2,138	1,442	2,138
STATE TAXES				
1ST TIER	300	300	288	300
2ND TIER	787	343	0	343
TOTAL	1,087	643	288	643

APPENDIX D-2

ESTIMATING SOCIAL
SECURITY BENEFITS

Chapter 7 presented a simplified method for estimating your Social Security benefits. This section presents more exact methods for calculating these Social Security benefits for retirement, disability, and survivorship. Read Chapter 7 before starting these calculations to be sure you are eligible for benefits.

Two terms must be identified at this point since they are essential for understanding Social Security benefits.

AIME   AVERAGE INDEXED MONTHLY EARNINGS. This is a figure developed from your history of earnings on which you paid Social Security taxes over your working lifetime. These are time consuming figures to develop yourself and can be obtained from the Social Security service.

PIA   PRIMARY INSURANCE AMOUNT This amount is determined from the AIME. This is the basic amount you would be eligible to receive each month. In most cases adjustments must be made to this basic amount for such things as age of retirement or maximum family benefit.

Each year there are cost of living

adjustments that result in increases in the maximum amount of earnings to be taxed, and in the indexing factors used in the AIME calculation. Therefore, any final information must be obtained from the Social Security office.

The methods presented here will be generally applicable to people reaching age 62 in 1992 and the following few years.

CALCULATION

AVERAGE INDEXED MONTHLY EARNINGS

An accurate calculation of this value requires the annual earnings on which you paid Social Security taxes from your first year of work up to the latest year of work. This can be obtained from your work records or from the Social Security Administration.

TABLE 5 D-2 at the end of this section is a work sheet that can be used to calculate the AIME for your particular situation. The index factors apply to a given year and account for the inflation up to that given date. This table has the factors in effect in 1992. If you are using this table for other years, you must update the factors for that year.

The number of years of earnings to be included in the calculation varies with your birth date as given in Table 1 D-2 for retirement, disability and survivor benefits.

TABLE 1 D-2

NUMBER OF YEARS COUNTED IN AIME

YEAR BIRTH	FOR RETIREMENT	FOR DISABILITY	FOR SURVIVOR
1917	23	23	23
1918	24	24	24
1919	25	25	25
1920	26	26	26
1921	27	27	27
1922	28	28	28
1923	29	29	29
1924	30	30	30
1925	31	31	31
1926	32	32	32
1927	33	33	33
1928	34	34	34
1929	35	35	35
1930	35	35	35
1931	35	34	34
1932	35	33	33
1933	35	32	32
1934	35	31	31
1935	35	30	30
1936	35	29	29
1937	35	28	28
1938	35	27	27
1939	35	26	26
1940	35	25	25
1941	35	24	24
1942	35	23	23
1943	35	22	22
1944	35	21	21
1945	35	20	20
1946	35	20	19
1947	35	19	18
1948	35	18	17
1949	35	17	16
1950	35	16	15

TABLE 3 D-2 (at the end of this section) has a column giving the maximum

taxed earnings for each year after 1951
including 1992. This table includes the
1992 multiplication factors that are used
to level the taxed rate to an equal
spending basis. These factors are
revised each year.

   The AIME calculation procedure is as
follows:

1. Put in your taxed earnings for each
    year up to the maximum on which tax
    is paid.
2. Estimate your earnings for the
    future years before age 65 if you
    intend to keep working to that age.
    Do not exceed the maximum taxed
    amount. If these years extend beyond
    1992 put in the last maximum for
    these years.
3. Multiply each year's earnings by
    the factor for that year.
4. From Table 1 D-2, use your year
    of birth to get the number of years
    to be used in the calculation.
5. Cross out the lowest year's
    earnings until you are left with
    number of year's earnings as in Step
    4.
6. Add up the figures for the
    required number of years.
7. Get the average monthly figure by
    dividing the total by the number of
    months in the years given in Step 4.
    For example if you were born in 1927
    you must use 33 yearly earning
    figures in the addition, and use 396
    months (12 x 33 = 396) in the
    division to get the average.

   This figure will be your AIME
(Average Indexed Monthly Earnings) and
will be used to calculate your benefits.

CALCULATION

PRIMARY INSURANCE AMOUNT (PIA)

The PIA is the amount you would receive each month if you retired at the normal retirement age. Currently this age is 65.

The basic PIA calculation is based on a person reaching age 62 in 1992. The PIA is 90% of the first $387 of AIME, 32% of the next $1,946 of AIME, and 15% above $2,333 of the AIME. The factors for other years are given in Table 2 D-2.

The calculations are more complicated for persons who are of different ages. Persons who reached 62 years of age before 1992, may estimate their PIA by using the information in the following table:

TABLE 2 D-2

PIA CALCULATION FACTORS

YEAR OF BIRTH	90% FIRST	32% NEXT	15% OVER	AIME INDEX MULTIPLIER
1930	$387	$1,946	$2,333	1.000000
1929	370	1,860	2,230	0.955848
1928	356	1,789	2,145	0.919444
1927	339	1,705	2,044	0.876285
1926	319	1,603	1,922	0.823751
1925	310	1,556	1,866	0.800006
1924	297	1,493	1,790	0.767314
1923	280	1,411	1,691	0.724713
1922	267	1,345	1,612	0.691048
1921	254	1,274	1,528	0.654989

The AIME index multiplier for the year of birth is used to get the new index factors. Multiply each year's index factor by the multiplier to get a new factor. An index factor cannot be below 1.000. The new AIME would then be calculated as in the stepwise procedure given above.

The PIA would then be calculated using the new increments given in Table 2 D-2. The resulting PIA must then be further adjusted by the cost of living factors given in Table 7-4 of Chapter 7. For example, if you became 65 in 1992, your year of birth was 1927 and you became 62 in 1989. The cost of living increases in the PIA are 1.037 x 1.054 x 1.047 or 1.1444 for the three years 1989, 1990, 1991.

The PIA is calculated from the AIME (Averaged Indexed Monthly Earnings) determined above. If a person became 62 years of age in 1992 the calculation is as follows using an example where the AIME was $2500.

```
90% of first $387 of AIME   = $ 348.30
32% of next $1,946 of AIME  = $ 622.72
15% of all above $2,333     = $  25.05
                               -----
                    PIA     = $  996.07
```

Table 3 D-2 shows the PIA for various values of the AIME. These values are for persons who reach 62 years of age in 1992 but retire at age 65.

TABLE 3 D-2

PIA FOR VARIOUS VALUES OF AIME

AIME	PIA	AIME	PIA
700	448	2,600	1,011
800	480	2,700	1,026
900	512	2,800	1,041
1,000	544	2,900	1,056
1,100	576	3,000	1,071
1,200	608	3,100	1,086
1,300	640	3,200	1,101
1,400	672	3,300	1,116
1,500	704	3,400	1,131
1,600	736	3,500	1,146
1,700	768	3,600	1,161
1,800	800	3,700	1,176
1,900	832	3,800	1,191
2,000	864	3,900	1,206
2,100	896	4,000	1,221
2,200	928	4,100	1,236
2,300	960	4,200	1,251
2,400	981	4,300	1,266
2,500	996	4,400	1,281
		4,500	1,296

Table 4 D-2 summarizes the benefits as a percentage of the PIA for the various types of benefit. There are special situations that may require rulings from the Social Security Administration.

TABLE 4 D-2

BENEFITS AS A PERCENTAGE OF PIA

RETIREMENT

Insured retiring at age 65	100%
Insured retiring at age 62	80
Spouse below age 62	0
Spouse age 62	37.5
Spouse age 65	50
Spouse with child under 16	50
Eligible child	50
Maximum family benefit	188

DISABILITY

Spouse age 65	50%
Spouse age 62	37.5
Spouse with child under 16	50
Eligible child	50
Maximum family benefit	150

SURVIVORS

Spouse age 65	100%
Spouse age 62	82.9
Disabled spouse, age 50-59	71.5
Spouse, under age 61 with eligible child	75
Each eligible child	75
Maximum family benefit	188

TABLE 5 D-2
CALCULATION TABLE
AVERAGE INDEXED MONTHLY EARNINGS
(AIME)

YEAR	MAXIMUM EARNINGS	YOUR EARNINGS	1992 FACTOR	YOUR FACTOR	INDEXED EARNINGS
1951	3600		7.51224		
1952	3600		7.07222		
1953	3600		6.69800		
1954	3600		6.66362		
1955	4200		6.36934		
1956	4200		5.95295		
1957	4200		5.77419		
1958	4200		5.72377		
1959	4800		5.45360		
1960	4800		5.24765		
1961	4800		5.14539		
1962	4800		4.90003		
1963	4800		4.78274		
1964	4800		4.59496		
1965	4800		4.51368		
1966	6600		4.25809		
1967	6600		4.03341		
1968	7800		3.77403		
1969	7800		3.56784		
1970	7800		3.39915		
1971	7800		3.23653		
1972	9000		2.94765		
1973	10800		2.77408		
1974	13200		2.61843		
1975	14100		2.43635		
1976	15300		2.27909		
1977	16500		2.15023		
1978	17700		1.99203		
1979	22900		1.83179		
1980	25900		1.68042		
1981	29700		1.52674		
1982	32400		1.44708		
1983	35700		1.37985		
1984	37800		1.30325		
1985	39600		1.24999		
1986	42000		1.21396		
1987	43800		1.14119		
1988	45000		1.08761		
1989	48000		1.04619		
1990	51300		1.00000		
1991	53400		1.00000		
1992	55500		1.00000		

APPENDIX D-3

INSURANCE CALCULATIONS

This section is an addendum to Chapter 9 on insurance. Three examples are presented on how you might calculate the amount of life insurance you need to assure that your spouse or heirs have sufficient funds to live out their lives in the event you die. The purchase of life insurance was assumed at the time of retirement.

These examples all assume that your savings are not as great as you would like. They also assume that the payments for insurance must come from your living expenses. The conclusion reached in all three examples is the cost of insurance is greater than the gain. Only in very unusual circumstances is the purchase of insurance after the time of retirement worthwhile.

EXAMPLE 1

Assume you and your spouse have earning assets of $500,000, and have no dependents. You are both 65 years old with a 25-year life expectancy. You have current living expenses of $50,000 per year including taxes, and are drawing social security payments of $15,000 per year. Your nest egg is drawing interest at 8% per year from Treasury Bonds. You would like to be assured your spouse has a reasonable income after your death.

Calculations are as in Chapter 5.

		ESCALATION	ANNUITY VALUE
YOUR NEED	$50,000	4%	$763,400
SOCIAL SECURITY	15,000	4	229,020
FROM SAVINGS	35,000	4	534,380

The need for savings is higher than that available so insurance seems to be in order. A further look may show it is not a wise move. A $50,000 whole life insurance policy would cost about $2,000 per year. The after-tax cost would be about $2,500. If you reduced your expenses by this same $2,500, the savings requirement would be as follows:

		ESCALATION	ANNUITY VALUE
YOUR NEED	$47,500	4%	$725,230
SOCIAL SECURITY	15,000	4	229,020
FROM SAVINGS	32,500	4	496,210

This example shows that cutting expenses will accomplish the same result as buying insurance.

EXAMPLE 2

Al is 65 years old and thinking seriously about retirement. His wife Betty, a homemaker, is 50 years old. His life expectancy is 20 years but hers is 40 years. Al would like to assure that Betty has sufficient funds to live out her life. Their financial situation is as follows:

```
                              TODAY'S DOLLARS
Estimated living cost              $40,000
Al's Social Security benefit         9,000
Al's pension                        20,000
From savings (first year)           11,000
    All the above escalate
    at inflation rate of 4%.
Their retirement nest egg is       $200,000
Betty will receive Soc. Sec.
    At age 65        (50%)           4,500
    At Al's death    (100%)          9,000
After Al's death, Betty can live
    on 75% of the joint costs       30,000
```

The need for life insurance can be calculated by setting up a table showing their situation for three different periods. The first is from today until Betty's 65 birthday. The second is from Betty's birthday until Al's death, assumed to be 20 years hence. The third period is from Al's death until the end of Betty's life, assumed to be 20 years.

```
                        Time periods, Years
                 0 - 15   15 -20   20 -40
Need (Today's dollars)
             $40,000  $40,000  $30,000

Income (Today's dollars)
  From Social
  Security        9,000   13,500    9,000
  From pension   20,000   20,000        0
  From savings   11,000    6,500   21,000
    (By difference)
```

These figures must be adjusted for inflation to give the values needed for the year at the beginning of the period.

From savings (inflated to first year of
  each period).

	Time periods, Years		
	0 - 15	15 -20	20 -40
	11,000	11,706	46,013
Factor	10,807	4,299	13,247
(From Appendix A-5, Table 2)			
Total savings needed for the period.	118,877	50,324	609,534

Since these values are the total
amount needed at the beginning of the
specific period they are are adusted to
give the amount needed today.

Total from savings, Today's dollars
First period   118,877
Second period   15,864
Third period   130,773
         Total $265,514

For the purposes here, it was
assumed that the money would earn 8%
interest util needed.

	Calculation of divisor	
Second period	$(1.08)^{15}$	= 3.1722
Third period	$(1.08)^{20}$	= 4.6610

The current dollars are calculated
from the dollars at later years by
dividing by the factors calculated above
or obtained from Appendix A-2. For
example, $130,773 invested at 8% interest
for 20 years becomes $609,534.

This shows the $200,000 is
inadequate for the plan given above. It
can be shown that modest lowering of the
expenditure plan can make insurance
unnecessary. This decrease of spending

will be less than the cost of the insurance. Assume the insurance would cost at least $2,000 per year over the 20-year life of Al. This money invested at 8% becomes $91,524. (Appendix A-3). This sum will provide an additional initial $6,909 per year to Betty's annual income after Al is gone. The $6,909 will increase at 4% per year sum and reach $15,138 in the 20th year at which point the principal will be exhausted. If Al dies before the 20 year life expectancy, Betty's need would drop and she would have sufficient funds.

Here, it is better for Al and Betty to reduce their standard of living by 5% ($2,000 per year) than to spend it on insurance. The expenditure of the money for insurance would lower the standard of living anyway.

EXAMPLE 3

Assume you and your spouse have assets of $500,000 invested at 8%. Your needs today are $50,000 per year. You and your spouse are 65 and drawing Social Security benefits. You have a disabled child (40 years of age) who is also drawing Social Security benefits. The total family benefits are $16,900 per year (1991). Your pension is fixed at $20,000 per year. You are drawing $23,100 from your nest egg this year. You feel you must provide for your disabled child after you are gone.

The child will receive on death of the primary insured a benefit of 75% of the PIA of the insured or $6,750 per year (today's dollars). As parents you feel that you should provide for the child since rising nursing home costs could reach $75,000 to $150,000 a year by the end of his/her life. You do not want this person to depend on Medicaid or the welfare system.

A table is set up very similar to that of Example 2 in Chapter 5 using the factors for 8% interest and 30 years life expectancy and 0 and 4% inflation.

		ESCALATION RATE	AMOUNT REQUIRED
1992 NEED	$50,000	4%	$847,100
SOCIAL SECURITY	16,900	4%	286,320
PENSION	20,000	0%	225,160
FROM SAVINGS (BY DIFFERENCE)		?%	335,620

If there were no need to leave a sum for the disabled child, the required sum is well below the $500,000 available.

To approximate how much of the initial retirement sum is available at any time requires more extensive calculations. A table was set up with ten-year increments covering the family needs. This table is complicated but will be clear if you can understand the difference between today's dollar and future dollars. The future dollar is today's dollar plus the interest it has drawn between today and the future. Both are used in this table.

Years after retirement	0	10	20	30
Total need per year	50,000	74,000	110,000	162,000
From Social Security	16,900	25,000	37,000	55,000
From pension	20,000	20,000	20,000	20,000
From savings	13,100	29,000	53,000	87,000
Estimated annual % (1) increase in need from savings over each 10-year period.	8	6	5	5

Requirement per $1,000 of savings need for period. (8% interest, 10 year) From Appendix A-5	9,259	8,525	8,184	8,184

Required per period (start of period)	121,292	247,225	433,752	712,008

Actual dollars (2) (start of period)	500,000	817,592	1,231,408	1,722,080

Note 1. The annual percent increase in amount required from savings is estimated by dividing the new figure from the old to give the 10 year increase. The annual increase is determined from Appendix A-2 at the 10-year level. For example: $29,000/$13,100 = 2.13   In A-2 at 10 years and 8% interest one finds the value 2.1589 that is close to 2.13. Thus, 8 % is a close estimate of the annual increase in need from savings.

Note 2. The actual dollars available after each period (the start of next period) is calculated by subtracting the period need from the amount available at the beginning of the period. This value is then escalated by the interest rate compounded for the length of the period. For example, the amount at the beginning of the second period is:

$$(\$500,000 - 121,292) \times (1.08)^{10}$$
$$= \$817,592.$$

It is now necessary to calculate if the availability of cash is sufficient to meet the needs of the child. To give some idea of the needs of the invalid child if the parents die, they set up a table as follows:

Years after retirement	0	10	20	30
Need, if parents died	25,000	44,800	80,200	143,600
(Escalate 6% per year)				
Soc. Sec. Disability	6,750	10,000	14,800	21,900
(Escalate 4% per year)				
Need from estate	18,250	34,800	65,400	121,700
(Escalates 7% per year)				
Requirement per 1,000	31,071(1)	24,351	16,977	8,883
(7% escalation and				
8% interest for life				
expectancy).				
Total required	567,046	847,414	1,110,296	1,081,061
Available (from	500,000	817,592	1,231,408	1,722,080
previous table).				

Note 1.   The figure of $31,071 is at 40 years, which is beyond the limit of the tables

This shows the amount of money required to support the child should the parents die at anytime is adequate. The sums during the first ten years or so are a little less than desired, but the odds of both parents dying during this ten year period is low.

CONCLUSIONS

The section showed how to determine the amount of life insurance needed to provide for your heirs. Except under unusual situations, life insurance is not needed. Reductions in spending equal to insurance premiums leave more of your nest egg intact. This larger nest egg serves as insurance.

INDEX

A

AIME (Average Indexed Monthly
  Earnings) definition   84,239
      Calculation   240
      Calculation procedure   242
      Definition   84,239
      Estimation   86
      Years earning counted   241
Annuity   16
  Commercial   134
      Life expectancy   144,146
      Life expectancy adjustment 148
      Tax example   148
  Definition   16,19
  Employee   134
      Cost basis   149
      No. of payments (tax basis) 149
      Tables   62
      Taxes   148
  Escalation of payments   17
  Present value of   16,17
  Tables   62,206-209
  Taxes   144
Assets   11
  By age group   171-173
  Cash equivalent   22
  Check list   14
  Entitlement   22,78
  Examples of cost   187
  Income generating   12,14
  Liquid   22
  Lists   23,24
  Net   11
  Non-liquid   22
  Non-productive, cost of owning 187-191
  Sample work sheet   23,24
  Total   11
  Total need   63

B

Balancing income/expenses   224
  Calculation   224
  Estimating gap   225
Balancing income/expense (continued)
  First years taxes   237
  Long term taxes   238
  First year taxes   237

C

Compound value
  Definition   200
  Table   203
  Use of table   18

D

Data Collection   36
Debt   14,15
Distributions, tax deferred   135
  After 70.5 years of age   142
  Before 59.5 years of age   135
  IRA   141
  Lump sum   137
    5 year averaging   139
    10 year averaging   139

E

Entitlements   16,69
Escalation, also see inflation   17
Expenses, also see Spending   45
  And income gap   59
  Balancing Examples   59
  Check list   46,54
  Evaluation of alternates   76-79
  Future   52
  Organization of data   46
  Reducing   69
  Reduction Goal   71
  Steps to reduce   70
  Tables   55,57
  Taxes   50
  Unexpected   49

H

Home 74
  Asset 74,185
  Move to lower priced 75
  Tax exclusion 153

I

Income 25
  Balancing 59
  Balancing examples 64,66
  By age group 169,171
  Estimated 32
  From bonds 166
  From investments 166
  From stock equities 167
  Need 63
  Organization of information 33,36
  Sample income statement 41,43
Inflation 7,60
  Compounded 61
  Historical 212
Inheritance 25,26
Insurance 119
  Automobile 120
    Cost factors 121
    Reduction opportunities 122
  Co-insurance 125
  Home 124
    Costs 124
  Life insurance 127
    Calculation of amount 248-256
    Amount needed 248-256
  Medical 101
    Costs 101
    Private plans 102
    Group 104
  Self insurance 125
Interest 8
  Bonds 213
  Compounding of 18

L

Life expectancy	29-31
Tables, overall U.S.	30-216
Joint and last survivor tables	217
For annuities taxes	218
Lump sum	137-141
Five-year average	139
Ten-year average	139
Ten-year average tax rate	220
Ten-year average tax table	221

M

Medicaid	113
Medical cost/insurance	8-101
Factors	105
Insurance costs	101
Policies	106-107
Private/company plans	102
National medical costs	114-116
Summary	116-117
Medicare	82,103,108
Eligibility	109
Part A	111
Part B	111
Medigap	112
Money	
Discretionary	40
How long it will last	32
Spend taxed first	38

N

Need	63
Nest egg, how long will it last?	32
Net worth, see assets	11

P

Pension	19
Defined benefit	27,160
Defined contribution	27,160
Early retirement	158
Escalation	20
Questions to ask	159
Value of	16,19

PIA (Primary Insurance Amount) 239
  Calculation 239
  Definition 239
  For values of AIME 245
Population trends 174
  By ages 174
  Ratio, women/men 176
Present value 16
Present value of an annuity 16,17
  Definition 201
  Escalation 207,209
  No escalation 206
Present value of $1.00 205
  Definition 201
  Table 205

R

References 195
Retirement
  Age 26
  Benefits (age) 28
  Early incentives offer 155
  Gap 59,69
  Incentives 157,161
  Insurance 81
  Medical incentives 157
Reverse Mortgage 185-186

S

Saving, time benefit 179-180
  Evaluation of alternatives 76
  Taxed versus tax deferred 177-178
Spending, also see expenses
  By age group 168
  Reduction goal 71
  Steps to lower 70
  Reduction opportunities 71-73
Social Security 81
  Benefit estimation 239
  Benefit decrease, no contributions 165
  Disability 81
    Amount 95-96
    Benefits 94-246
    Eligibility 94
    Insurance 81

Disability (Continued)
   Maximum family   96
   Restrictions   96
   Table   246
   Years counted in calculation   241
Retirement benefits   82
   AIME   84
   Amount   82,87
   Calculation form   247
Retirement benefits (Continued)
   Cost of living increase   87
   Earnings while drawing   92
   Early retirement   88
   Eligibility   82
   Divorced spouse   91
   Family   90
   Late retirement   89
   Military service   93
   PIA   84,93,239,143
   Simplified calculation   84
   Special minimum   89
   Table, function of PIA   246
   Value of waiting to 65   163,221
   Years counted in calculation   241
Survivor insurance   81
   Calculation of amount   100
   Currently insured   99
   Eligibility   97
Survivor insurance (continued)
   Fully insured   98
   Lump sum death   100
   Maximum family benefit   100
   Table   246
   Years counted in calculation   241
Stocks, historical returns   214
Sum of an annuity   200
  Table   204
T
Taxes   131
  Annuities   144
  Deferred benefits   177

Deferred plans   132
   Annuities, see annuities   134,144
   Company   134
   IRA   133,141
   401 (K)   133
   Keogh   133
   SEP   134
   SERP   134
   Rules for taxing   135-137
Deferred versus taxed   37,181
Home sale exclusion   153
Lump sum   137-141
   Five-year average   139
   Ten-year average   139
   Ten-year average tax rate   220
   Ten-year average tax table   221
Spend taxed money first   38
Social Security, taxes on   150
   Calculation example   152
Ten-year average   219
   Table for 10-year average   220